The Book of the
MERCHANT NAVY PACIFICS

A British Railways Illustrated Special

By Richard Derry

First published in the United Kingdom in 2001
by Irwell Press Limited
59A, High Street, Clophill,
Bedfordshire MK45 4BE
Printed in Malta by Interprint

> **DEDICATION**
> I would like to dedicate these pages to the
> memory of a dear friend and fellow enthusiast,
> ## Graham Ward.

Acknowledgements

This book would not have been possible without the kind assistance of several people who, through their combined efforts, have seen to the thoroughgoing 'rebuilding' of my original manuscript, while retaining of course, all the best features of the original. My thanks especially to Eric Youldon, sometimes lonely torch bearer for the original engines but now winning the argument, and to Mark Arscott of Markits (all your 4mm requirements, especially Bulleid wheels! PO Box 40, Watford, Herts, WD24 6TN, tel/fax 01923 249711). Thanks also to Barry Fletcher, D.W. Winkworth, Hamish Stevenson, Chris Hawkins, Ian Sixsmith, John Fry, Alec Swain, Geoff Goslin, Brian Seddon, Martin Smith of *Railway Bylines* magazine, Alan Hammond and Barry Hoper of the inestimable Transport Treasury. The latter is probably an unrivalled source of postcard prints for the collector and modeller – write with s.a.e. to Gate House, North Road, Insch, Aberdeenshire, AB52 6XP; tel. and fax. 01464 820863.

Photograph below. Original 35021 NEW ZEALAND LINE at Loco Junction, Nine Elms 6 September 1958, moving up to Waterloo. The shed approach roads are on the right. R. C. Riley.

Contents

Bibliography

Bulleid's Pacifics by D.W. Winkworth (George Allen & Unwin, 1974 – original and amusing; thought provoking), *Locomotives of the Southern Railway Part 2* by D.L. Bradley (RCTS, 1976 – authoritative and painstaking; every facet laid out), *Loco Profile No.22* by Brian Reed (Profile Publications, 1972 – excellent introduction and thorough outline. Why oh why did they stop publishing them – it was the best 45p you could spend!), *British Pacific Locomotives* by Cecil J. Allen (Ian Allan 1962; broad sweep *par excellence*), *Master Builders of Steam* by H.A.V. Bulleid (Ian Allan 1963; one of the best loco reads there are – with a preface by Bulleid, Ivatt and Stanier!), *Bulleid of the Southern,* another great work by the same author more than a decade later; *Bulleid Power – The Merchant Navy Class* by A.J. Fry (Alan Sutton 1990; puts the C in Comprehensive). Beyond this, there have been umpteen articles from the mainstream railway press since the 1940s, from the *Railway Magazine* to the *Railway Observer* and SLS *Journal*. Bulleid, like Gresley, even has his own Society with a magazine devoted to his works – *The Leader*. Vastly detailed accounts still appear today even in modelling magazines in which the fine old art of 'engine picking' is raised to sublime heights – to levels in fact, that I can only grasp at. I think I have added something at least to the tale, and I think readers will agree, for such material as is retained at the NRM and Kew has been consulted and a few nuggets garnered from the professional press of the time, *The Railway Gazette, Railway Engineer, Southern Railway Magazine* and so on.

A somewhat down-at-heel 21C2 UNION CASTLE, still with brass gunmetal plates, stands outside Exmouth Junction shed in 1949. The rather home-grown looking ACE board was an early design made from sheet metal, used for several named trains on the SR. Three sand filler hatches by now, one for each wheel. It bore the gunmetal plates until renumbered and painted blue in early 1950; the Flaman speed recorder was put on in 1945 for test runs Waterloo-Bournemouth. Hinged inspection cover (for access to mechanical lubricators as they were then sited) open in front of smokebox. Photograph W. Hermiston, The Transport Treasury.

'Ten New Main Line Locomotives'

Scarcely can a railway board have entered on such a time of frustrating maintenance work, disappointing performance, lows mixed with thrilling highs, uncertainty, expense and worry with such an innocuous phrase – *'Ten New Main Line Locomotives'*. They were two sides of a coin, the Merchant Navy Pacifics – love 'em, hate 'em, scorn versus adulation; seldom could the phrases 'brilliant steaming' be conjoined so often with 'heavy maintenance', or the words 'exhilarating performance' with 'caught fire'*.

It might be that the Merchant Navy Pacifics are the most difficult British express locomotives to write about. The Duchesses, Royal Scots and Princesses and even the BR Standards which have formed the subject of previous 'Books of' in this series enjoyed a fairly consistent perception among enthusiasts and professionals alike. With the products of Bulleid it was different – the opposite in fact was the case. Where one person saw a sublime virtue, another saw a sorry handicap. Even today feelings can run high…

Whichever side of the divide you stand, it is clear that the Merchant Navys (how do you *spell* the plural even, Navys or Navies?) were not an ordinary class of passenger steam locomotive. Contradiction seems to have been their middle name from the very first. Even when introduced at the height of the Second World War for instance, these locomotives – plainly express Pacifics to anyone with eyes – were classified

Mixed Traffic. This is how Bulleid, it has often been said, was able to sneak them past the men at the ministry, overcoming material restrictions and shortages (in fact, not the least heroic part of the whole tale is how Bulleid ever got them built at the time he did). Yet the description, arrived at in 1938 for the benefit of the SR Board, *was true*; Merchant Navys, at least at first and in part, were thoroughly 'mixed traffic' in the way they were worked. On the West of England runs, if not particularly elsewhere, they always had booked turns on perishables, milk and stopping trains.

In fact the suggestion regarding devious 'mixed traffic' labelling has become something of a 'rubber stamp' over the years and needs amending. For instance, the Nine Elms Merchant Navy that worked down on the 3.0pm off Waterloo returned on the 10.42pm freight from Exeter Central Yard to Nine Elms Goods for years – and that's just one example.

So, it is clear that the whole history of the Merchant Navy Pacifics was almost designed for contention, for having taken the path of unconventionality and individuality with all the controversy it threw up, they were then abruptly and completely reconstituted, into as conventional a steam locomotive as you could wish for. Along the way every detail variation that it was possible to explore and utilise was so explored and utilised, leaving the class an engine-picker's paradise, and a

minefield for those who prefer certainty in life.

I have, sadly. no choice but to approach the subject largely from the (increasingly) middle-aged armchair enthusiast's point of view but I hope to have injected some of the youthful trainspotter's wonder at these mighty machines – a trainspotter, moreover, who grew up within sight and sound of the Western Section main line of the Southern Region, eyes wide at the daily succession of roaring Pacifics – yea, even the very last of the originals.

Bulleid and Modernising the Southern Steam Stock

The class appeared at a time of war, so there was little of the publicity that the LNER A4 streamliners and LMS Pacifics attracted in the 1930s – more significantly there was no series of well-publicised speed runs, or romantic new services. There was no 'Silver Jubilee' for Bulleid's first Pacific, and no stage on which to shine. This was a pity as the technical innovations together with unconventional appearance deserved more.

Bulleid, born in Invercargill at the southern tip of the South Island of New Zealand, served a premium apprenticeship at Doncaster. To summarise his career in a few words, he rose to be Gresley's Assistant on the

*One has to be careful here – there *were* fires on Merchant Navys, it is true, but they were comparatively rare. It was the light Pacifics that particularly suffered in this regard.

CHANNEL PACKET, almost 'as built', but with front numberplate lowered, and the three lower lamps raised – effectively swopping positions since building. There was only one footstep at first, on the nearest side, but a second one (as here) was soon added, also slung under the buffer. Front steps were afterwards always arranged so. Photograph Collection E.S. Youldon.

On 10 March 1941 CHANNEL PACKET was named at Eastleigh by Lord Brabazon. Afterwards 21C1 hauled a three coach guest special to Alresford on the Mid-Hants line where it is seen soon after arrival. His Lordship, with peaked cap, can be spotted among the admirers talking to Bulleid. The engine retains the unlucky horseshoe and has the three bottom lamps and the number plate on original site. These items later swopped positions.

Great Northern and accounts of his days there, during the momentous times of the Pacifics, 10000 and the Mikados, the Vitry Testing Station and so on make rewarding reading, in *Master Builders of Steam* for instance, by H.A.V. Bulleid (Ian Allan, 1963) and *Bulleid: Last Giant of Steam* by Sean Day-Lewis (George Allen & Unwin, 1963). By the 1930s Bulleid was

probably the most prominent 'No.2' on the Big Four and a sudden approach from Sir Herbert Walker of the Southern Railway is said to have come 'out of the blue'. The post of CME of the Southern was his if he cared to apply for it. He did and was appointed and was at his desk in the Waterloo offices in September 1937, a matter of a few months after Walker's approach.

Steam had been neglected on the Southern in favour of electrification and even by 1936 electric train mileage was easily exceeding steam. Yet the longer routes on the former London & South Western Railway were still steam hauled and the heavy boat trains on the Eastern Section still required the best that was available in steam power. The steam stock

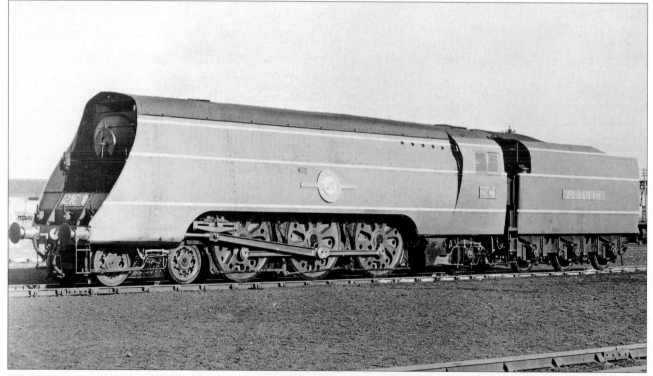

Original condition, March 1941 – metal plates, matt malachite, three yellow lines and that glorious 'widow's peak' as it's often described in the literature. (It is actually the opposite of a widow's peak – but it sounds good.) Note also slightly larger 'C'.

Preparations going ahead for this volume in 1999-2000 prompted Eric Youldon to an account of the Bulleid valve gear, a more sympathetic ('balanced' he would say) than can usually be found in published accounts. This first appeared in our parent magazine *British Railways Illustrated* in its April 2000 issue. What follows is a slightly amended version:

BULLEID'S CHAIN DRIVEN VALVE GEAR
Some Notes by Eric Youldon

When O.V.S. Bulleid came to draw up his specification for new main line locomotives in the late thirties he was influenced by the amount of time that drivers spent in pits oiling inside gear in conditions that were invariably appalling. He therefore concluded that inside motion should be enclosed and be self-oiling. He also reasoned this would ensure that working parts were protected from dirt and therefore the need for attention between works visits would be minimal. He did concede that when attention was necessary, access problems would arise.

Early thoughts were focussed on a Caprotti drive but wartime material shortages and dependence on an outside supplier ruled this out and so Bulleid decided to develop and patent his own design of valve gear, enclosed in an oil bath. Three cylinder Pacifics were ultimately designed and so the middle connecting rod, crosshead and slidebars were also accommodated within the bath. Any notion (sometimes expressed) that the enclosed mechanism thrashed about wildly in a bath full of oil can be dispelled immediately; the oil level amounted to just eight inches, as shown on the diagram. The only churning effect was caused by the three-throw crankshaft.

The Railway Gazette diagram shows the main features of the layout that was used for the Southern Pacifics built 1941-51, which involved a Morse chain drive to a three-throw crankshaft. The initial drive was from the centre coupled axle to an intermediate sprocket and was horizontal to allow for rise and fall of the engine on its springs. The shaft of this sprocket had a second sprocket that drove a further chain extending downwards to a final sprocket mounted on the three-throw crankshaft. Each crank of the latter operated a set of valve gear – one for each piston valve – and its three cranks were spaced out accordingly. Each valve gear consisted of two elements; from the crankpin a vertical eccentric rod rocked the expansion link controlling the radius rod. From the lower end of the eccentric rod a short forward extension was coupled to the combination lever via the union link. These elements corresponded to the eccentric rod and crosshead drives of a conventional set of Walschaerts gear.

The combination lever actuated a plunger linked to the valve rod connected at the other end to the piston valve rocker shaft. Connection to the valve was effected in the centre of the steam chest, which was the exhaust compartment as the cylinders were of the outside admission type.

The intermediate sprocket shaft was adjustable to some extent so that a degree of chain slack could be taken up. The crankshaft had a small sprocket and simple chain drive that operated a pair of pumps for distributing oil at about 20lb/sq.in. from a forty gallon sump. Delivery was by means of a series of small bore pipes that sprayed the working parts and also fed the rubbing surfaces of the inside slidebars. Reversing and cut-off adjustment was effected by steam reverser. The whole gear was small and light in weight and this helped make for free running – one of these engines' characteristics.

Chain stretch beyond the limit of adjustment was obviously an undesirable weakness, but did not affect the length of valve travel, although valve events could be influenced. The whole assembly was a challenge to fitters if the engines (there were 140 of them) were to be kept in good order, but with the backup of a good team of fitters a depot such as Exmouth Junction with some forty Bulleids on its books would daily turn out its Packets and West Countries with the same confidence as their S15s, Woolworths, T9s, Standard Tanks and all the rest.

The question that has to be asked is 'Were the designer's aims realised?' The answer is, yes and no. Simplicity in preparation of working parts was undoubtedly achieved and was much appreciated by many drivers, as revealed in the 'Pistell Testimonial', a collection of highly laudatory and appreciative statements assembled by Driver Pistell in 1966 and presented to Bulleid on his retirement. On the other side of the coin, freedom from fitters' attention was not to be enjoyed on the scale intended and oil bath dismantling was resorted to from time to time, although there is little evidence that this significantly reduced mileages covered once early problems had been overcome. Failures out on the road occasionally took place and sometimes with spectacular results but it should be borne in mind that 'ordinary' locomotives had their quota of serious motion failures too. Oil soaked lagging fires were a problem never eradicated which is surprising because the covering of the lagging by sheeting would surely have done the trick.

On the credit side, overheating of the inside big end and main journals of the centre coupled wheels was very rare – there was no need for a heat detector (the 'stink bomb') provided for the middle big end of the ninety locomotives later rebuilt on conventional lines.

When Bulleid heard, in 1956, that the prototype rebuild 35018 was experiencing overheating problems he penned a letter to R.C. Bond (CME, BTC) suggesting he might consider an oilbath but, presumably for diplomatic reasons, it wasn't sent!

The design, it was said, was 'experimental' and intended for goods service too... Denied the usual publicity outlets, the Southern had a fair go in its own organ, *Southern Railway Magazine,* under the bald (and bold) headline *'BIG NEW STREAMLINED ENGINE FOR SOUTHERN'.*

'A new Southern Railway locomotive of a striking and original design is being introduced into the service. It is the first streamlined – or, as its designer, Mr. O.V. Bulleid, the Company's Chief Mechanical Engineer, prefers 'air smoothed' locomotive of the Southern Railway. The new engine was formally named 'Channel Packet' by the Minister of Transport, Lt. Col. J.T.C. Moore Brabazon, MC at Eastleigh Works on March 10th and is one of ten which will be known as the Merchant Navy Class, to remind the public of the Southern's close association with the Mercantile Marine. The succeeding engines will be named after famous shipping lines associated with the Southampton Docks as their home port.'

There was no mention at this stage of the merchant seaman, for which the naming policy was later claimed. The ten engines were 'being built experimentally' for heavy express passenger and goods services. Besides being the first streamlined Southern Railway engine – apart from the makeshift efforts applied to a Schools in 1938 – CHANNEL PACKET was also *the first English locomotive to have electric lighting, both for head and tail code lamps and for the gauges and inspection lights in the driver's cabin'.* It is not clear if this was just the customary slip of 'English' for 'British' or whether some Scottish or Irish locomotives had once carried electric lights.

'At the naming of 'Channel Packet', the Minister of Transport was accompanied by the Southern Railway Chairman, Mr. R. Holland-Martin, and the General Manager, Mr. E.J. Missenden, together with other Directors and Chief Officers of the Company, officials from the Ministry of Transport, and representatives of the press and news reels. After the naming ceremony Lt. Col. Moore Brabazon, in driver's peak cap, black mackintosh and gloves, drove the locomotive along some sidings to a train, to which it was then attached for a trial run. With him in the cabin was Driver Tate (noted as the King and Queen's driver when Their Majesties travel on the Southern). Giving his opinion on the new engine, Lt. Col. Moore Brabazon said that he thought it was lovely and that Mr. O.V. Bulleid who had designed it, was not only an engineer but an artist.'

needed updating, an opportunity in which Bulleid saw more scope for experimentation and innovation than the average, unsuspecting, SR Board member could dream of. Turntable and track considerations soon ruled out 4-8-2s or 2-8-2s so a Pacific it would have to be. Not a 'conventional express passenger engine' to be sure but, as H.A.V. Bulleid puts it, one which could be more aptly described as 'fast mixed traffic'. People have been arguing over the wording ever since. This was in 1938, and the Merchant Navy Pacifics began to grow from a Board agreement to a rather harmless-looking requirement for 'ten new main line steam locomotives'. There was no one on the Board that day who could have thought for the merest second that one day the Southern would have more Pacifics than the LMS!

The second Merchant Navy, repeating most of 21C1's early features, on a four coach test special at Merstham, 4 July 1941. Light under the 'widow's peak' shows the square hole cut round the chimney.

The locomotive's numbering was of course odd to the British eye and 21C1 had to be explained: *'The number, according to the new "Southern" notation, gives the number of the engine,* *whilst at the same time, the wheel arrangement is indicated. The number of driving axles is indicated by the corresponding letter of the alphabet e.g. C for three.'* It did not quite make so much sense to everyone else of course; not only was it misleading because every other working locomotive in the country had a more familiar, traditional type of number, the system

The first two boilers on their way from NBL at Glasgow to Eastleigh for completion and fixing. They have regulator handles for both driver's and fireman's side – so the latter could close it promptly in an emergency. The fireman's side regulator (it seems only to have gone on the first boiler or so) was later removed. Photograph Collection John Fry.

did not even have the doubtful virtue of following continental practice; but then, in 1941 after all, few Britons were going to have much to do with Europe in the near future in any conventional sense... The letter notation as used in Europe utilised letters for the number of coupled axles and numbers for front and rear axles, so a 4-6-0 was 2C0, a 2-8-2 141 and a Pacific 2C1. As it turned out, Southern railwayman (as well as local enthusiasts) took to the strange notation perfectly readily; the engines after all were so different from anything else that a conventional number almost 'wouldn't do!

The new locomotive, it could not be denied, incorporated plenty of 'new features'. These were summarised as follows:

(a) Streamlining; another and more accurate description would be 'air smoothed'. The casing enclosing the

engine is carried on the main frame instead of on the boiler, as is usually done, and the boiler, consequently, is free to expand inside it. The casing is fabricated by electric welding from rolled sections and one-sixteenth inch steel sheet.

(b) The cab is a continuation of the air-smoothed casing and, like it, is carried on the frame.

(c) The casing forward of the smokebox doorplate acts as an air collector. The large opening over the smokebox door forms the mouth of a funnel tapering to a narrow slot in front of the chimney, discharging a stream of air upwards at high velocity, acting as a screen to the exhaust.

(d) The enclosed space between the frames in front of the smokebox holds the electric light turbo-generator and two mechanical lubricator pumps. This engine is the first English locomotive to be completely lighted by electricity, as both the head and tail lamps are so lighted, in addition to the gauges and the lamps fitted for inspection purposes.

(e) All the cast steel wheel centres, both engine and tender, are the new double-disc patent BFB type.

(f) The driving wheels are fitted with clasp brakes i.e. each wheel has a brake block on each side.

(g) Cab fittings. Both injectors are fitted on the firemen's side, the steam and water controls being arranged in one group on the cab side. The reversing gear is power operated, the steam and hydraulic cylinders being controlled by a single lever.

(h) The tender above the frame is all welded, the profile of the sides being the same as that of the latest 'Southern' carriages. Clasp brakes are fitted to the wheels operated by four 21 inch cylinders through automatic slack adjusters. The tender is filled through covers in the tender cab end at each side, thereby making it unnecessary for the fireman to climb on to the top of the tender.

(i) The boiler – the internal firebox is of steel and is fitted with two thermic syphons. The inner and outer fireboxes are welded. Automatic fire hole doors are fitted. The boiler is lagged with spun glass mattresses.

(j) Valve gear – the Bulleid patent radial valve gear is fitted. The three sets are enclosed in an oil tight casing inside the frames which also encases the middle connecting rod, crosshead and crank. All bearings within this casing are lubricated by a continuous stream of oil pumped by gear pumps from the sump.

Photograph bottom left. Those exotic 'box section', 'boxpok' or 'BFB' wheels; a set from the first batch at Eastleigh, in 1941. Bulleid spurned proprietary models of this American-type wheel that were available, coming up with cast steel centres. 'BFB' stands for 'Bulleid-Firth-Brown', the latter two names representing the involvement of the Sheffield steel firm of Thomas Firth and John Brown. According to the patent abstract published in *The Railway Gazette* of 16 May 1941, the patent specification for 'B.F.B.' wheels bears the name of Thomas Beaumont and Joseph Fenwick Bridge, both of the Atlas Works, Sheffield, with no mention of Bulleid. So maybe they are actually 'Beaumont-Fenwick-Bulleid' wheels! It matters not – the point is they saved something more than ten per cent in weight and performed well; the rim was shrunk on and secured to the hub not by pins and keys but by a continuous annular corrugated web. They seem to have attracted no criticism and were of course retained in the rebuilt locomotives.
Photograph Collection John Fry.

It might seem clear that, from the first, the engines were named after the great shipping lines that were so

SOUTHERN RAILWAY MAGAZINE

with which is incorporated
THE SOUTH WESTERN GAZETTE
(first issued 1881)

Vol. XIX. No. 219.   *Nov.-Dec., 1941.*

NAMED IN HONOUR OF OUR—   ROYAL MAIL   —BRAVE MERCHANT SEAMEN !

MERCHANT   **NAVY CLASS**

intimately connected with the Southern and its services but it was not so. According to Bradley in *Locomotives of the Southern Railway Part Two* (RCTS 1976) it had been intended that the engines carry British victories of the Second World War. By 1941, sadly, these were not that numerous although a trial plate was made commemorating the sinking of the *Graf Spee*. Later, various capitals of Britain and the Empire were considered but these didn't get anywhere either. It was, Bradley relates, actually the suggestion of the Union Castle Chairman to use merchant shipping lines. Before long someone realised that as everyone was supposed to be in it together the workers ought not to feel left out. 21C1 was already incorporated in the *Southern Magazine* title page but by the time of the third Merchant Navy the engines were being named to mark the (often ultimate) contribution of the merchant seaman keeping the country supplied with food and materials: witness the accompanying illustration above.

The first Merchant Navy had three cylinders, one less than the Lord Nelson and thereafter Bulleid departed from most contemporary practice. It is more or less impossible to have a satisfactory Walschaerts motion for an inside cylinder driving the centre axle, whether the valve is set on the top or at the side. (Standard Walschaerts motion could not be accommodated between the frames to drive the second coupled axle because the leading coupled axle was in the way.) Bulleid

did not want divided drive, and he did not want Gresley conjugated gear. He arrived at a separate three-throw crankshaft which allowed all three sets of valve gear to be enclosed in an oil bath, with the projected abolition of the daily preparation time at sheds and less maintenance. He wanted to drive this crankshaft by gears and a propeller shaft as in the rotary-cam poppet valve gears of Caprotti and Lentz but this could not be done because the necessary items were not available – Bulleid doubtless tired of the phrase 'There's a war on'.

So it was that the engines ended up with an enclosed oil bath, as intended, but with *chain driven* valve motion (the aforesaid 'Bulleid patent radial valve gear'). But, however damned the oil bath novelty has become (rightly or wrongly) in retrospect the attractions, *if such a thing could be made to work*, were obvious.

The economics of steam locomotive working were changing rapidly; together with coal quality it was the cost of labour that weighed so heavily against it. Bulleid could, in a way, perhaps be thought prescient in seeking to save the labour of servicing, for the enclosed oil bath would obviate the need for the driver to oil the gear every trip (and save the damage if it were not done properly) at a time of acute labour shortage. It would not be difficult to put a powerful case for the gear, adding up the daily minutes spent oiling and preparing and multiplying it across a sizeable fleet of locos, over an entire year. What Bulleid was

actually doing, however, was 'writing a long letter on a short piece of paper' and the designs meant to *reduce* labour ended by causing *more* labour than if purely conventional gear had been used. The Bulleid Pacifics are fertile ground for any student of the law of unintended consequences...

Another point to consider when trying to come to a verdict on these brilliant locomotives was the way Bulleid shoe-horned them into a very demanding weight and clearance profile. It must be remembered that they were designed with the Eastern Section boat trains in mind and over there weight and clearance restrictions were formidable. Maximum height above rails was 13ft. 1in. and maximum widths were 9ft. over the cab and 8ft. 10in. across the cylinders. The height of the cab cornice above the rail was 10ft. 11in. As Allen wrote in *British Pacific Locomotives*, 'No other British Pacific design has been subject to such drastic restrictions', and perhaps we should bear it more in mind.

Notable departures were the high pressure 280lb boiler and the welded steel firebox, and the use of thermic syphons. With the unusually high pressure Bulleid was hoping to emulate the sort of superheat limits (400 degrees C) advocated by Chapelon and with the steel firebox he was seeking savings in weight and cost. Eastleigh works, it seems, did not have the wherewithal to construct either of these items, the boilers or the fireboxes; there were certainly delays in getting the designs finally ready and, unpropitiously for Bulleid, drawings were not complete (the work was done at Brighton) until the final weeks of peace. Bulleid had to give the first order, for ten boilers and fireboxes, to an outside contractor, North British, and only on 19 August 1939, perilously late.

It was obviously not a good time to place any major engineering order; war was seen as inevitable, with who knew what horrors in store, from gas to mass bombing, and the Government was increasingly taking hold of industry and transport. It was here, doubtless, that the 'mixed traffic' classification of the engines came in useful – though perhaps we should not make *too* much of this. Remember the LMS could continue to build unashamedly passenger Pacifics despite wartime difficulties, and these included fully streamlined members of the class, awkward to work on in everyday service even in peacetime – see the earlier volume in this series *The Book of the Coronation Pacifics*.

Bulleid desired that the boilers should eventually be built at Eastleigh and according to Brian Reed (*Loco Profile No.22, Merchant Navy Pacifics*, Profile Publications Ltd, 1972) by the summer of 1940 he was pressing for suitable machinery, at a cost of £20,000 or more. Reed rather disapproved of Bulleid's activities and deprecated this sort of expenditure at

such a time of national need. They would not be available until May 1941, so in November 1940 another ten Merchant Navy boilers were ordered from North British – an order that was cancelled as Eastleigh acquired the necessary equipment and NBL proved ever more taken up with war work. It is not easy to deliver a verdict on such events all these years on. Government control in wartime might very well be a right and proper thing, but it didn't mean such a system was flawless – indeed it was probably a disruptive disaster in many spheres, especially in the first years. Bulleid, it could be said, triumphed against the odds, getting the engines he needed for his railway – which, after all, was in the Front Line like no other. In any event, the ten boilers ordered from NBL, for the first Merchant Navy Pacifics, eventually left the Hyde Park works and made their way to Eastleigh on specialised LNER wagons, from the end of 1940 to spring the following year.

These first ten boilers had the taper on the underside, on the front ring, with the rear ring parallel. They were riveted in their construction, with the case being welded. Whatever were the subsequent complaints about Bulleid's Pacifics, there was no doubt that the boiler was a truly prodigious steamraiser – 'generally recognised as the best of all Pacific boilers' as H.A.V. Bulleid puts it.

Bulleid felt the copper firebox, with its burden of maintenance, had had its day; welded steel fireboxes after all had been commonplace in the USA for years. The techniques and material (a suitable mild steel amenable to welding) were well tried and copper fireboxes both weighed and cost more than their steel counterparts. (A welded steel firebox saved 1½ tons over a riveted copper box.) X-ray inspection provided a safety insurance.

The fireboxes had two thermic syphons. These improved circulation but Bulleid's main concern, it seems, was a greater safety margin when water was low. Pressure, at 280lb/sq.in. was, after all, very high. (It was this high in order to limit the cylinder size and reciprocating weight in that restricted space below, while keeping the required high tractive effort).

When the news came that the second batch of ten NBL boilers ordered in November 1940 could not be made because of Government requirements, construction was transferred to Eastleigh where, as noted above, suitable equipment had now been made available. Beyer-Peacock once again provided the thermic syphons, work commencing on the ten new boilers in February 1944. Lack of staff and the job of familiarising them with the complicated new techniques delayed completion until the autumn.

Front bogie and driving wheel at Eastleigh in February 1941; in the background is the engine, 21C1. Photograph Collection John Fry.

CHANNEL PACKET taking shape – note the splashers, invisible hereafter and rumoured to be (largely) dispensed with on 21C3-21C10. Photograph Collection John Fry.

The first NBL boilers with the front ring tapering on the underside and the rear ring parallel (again, as noted above) were numbered 1090-1099. Eastleigh's version (1100-1124) had a parallel front and tapered rear ring – representing a further weight saving without reducing the steam surface heating area.

There were in total thirty-five boilers for the class, ten from NBL,

thirteen from Eastleigh (1100-1112) with the remainder (1113-1124) built at Brighton.

The original NBL fireboxes all suffered severe cracking in the throatplate, around the thermic syphon connections and around the stay holes in the backplate by the firehole door. It was here that scale tended to build up. Heat was at its fiercest at these points – precisely where the firebox body needed water to circulate the most freely, and it was here, un-fortunately, that water circulation was impaired by scale the most. Changing the stays to monel metal (a robust alloy) alleviated the leaking, while the syphons were modified by a separate 'diaphragm', welded around each of the syphon holes.

Untreated feed water, as was comprehensively used with the steel boxes in America, was a principal culprit in the firebox damage and the problems faded when new Eastleigh boxes were substituted, with TIA treatment. Just as deleterious, as had been found in America much earlier, was the washing out of hot boilers and fireboxes with cold water and the consequent rapid contraction. This, too, without allowing for a proper 'cooling-off period' would also encourage cracking and leaks. Instructions were issued that all locos were to stand for twelve hours before commencing a cold water washout.

Firebox life was greatly extended thereafter. Hot water washout, presumably, was the ultimate (American) solution and Bulleid would have been familiar with it from a number of installations on the LNER. He would certainly have thought of it, but no plants seem to have been installed. A couple of elderly locos, a 4-4-0 and an 0-4-2 at Salisbury and Exmouth Junction were provided to supply steam after washouts but these were abandoned after a while as effectively useless.

Bulleid recounted his firebox experiences in *The Railway Gazette* of 21 December 1945 (by which time twenty Merchant Navys were in service): '*Steel fireboxes were said to be unsatisfactory, because of the plates cracking. Copper fireboxes, however, are not immune from this trouble. There has been no experience of steel fireboxes in England in recent years, although it was known that firebox steel plate had improved in quality.*

'*A special firebox plate manufactured by one steelmaker has been found to be better than anything available previously ... and this new plate is almost free from creep – a great merit. It is readily weldable; and a completely welded inner and outer firebox was a practical possibility, in view of electric welding developments. As riveted joints*

21C8, not named as yet, on a train from the West of England at Surbiton in 1942, with LSW stock on the front. Engine is 'as built', with large 'C'; an indifferent photograph but one of exceptional rarity. Photograph Collection E.S. Youldon.

would be suppressed, there would be no double thickness of metal to cause trouble through overheating and burning away. Moreover, should cracks develop, there would be no difficulty in cutting out the defective piece of plate and welding in a new piece in situ.

'The use of steel instead of copper would greatly reduce weight – at least 1½ tons in the present case.

'The boilers of the first ten locomotives were built by the North British Locomotive Co. Ltd.; [here Bulleid acknowledged his indebtedness to Mr Lorimer and Mr Black of that firm for help in their design and manufacture]. Subsequent boilers have been produced at Eastleigh. The boiler and firebox are illustrated in Fig 1. [This is reproduced here.] All the

plates of the outer firebox, comprising back plates, wrapper, throat plate, and tube plate, are also welded together, the top flanges of both syphons being welded to the firebox roof. The inner and outer fireboxes are welded together at the firehole.

'For practical reasons the inner firebox has to be inserted through the foundation ring opening, and the shape of the inner firebox has to be checked to ensure that this is possible. All holes in the pressed plates are drilled before assembly. Wrappers are drilled on the flat before bending, as are barrel plates before rolling – an advance in technique which has quickened production considerably. The foundation ring, double-riveted throughout, is welded from four pieces.'

The first ten NBL fireboxes were all condemned at between four and six years' life during 1946-47, at somewhere around 200,000 miles, but with water treatment and washout care the second steel fireboxes fitted to the early boilers and those carried by 1110-1124 lasted the remaining life of the class. After that, boiler or firebox problems hardly ever caused a Merchant Navy to come out of service for repairs. After Nationalisation, the reduction in working pressure from 280 to 250lb/sq.in. was probably a contributory factor in prolonging their life. 35005, it could be noted, still carries NBL (1095) in preservation.

A 'Packet' Launched

21C1 was first steamed, at Eastleigh,

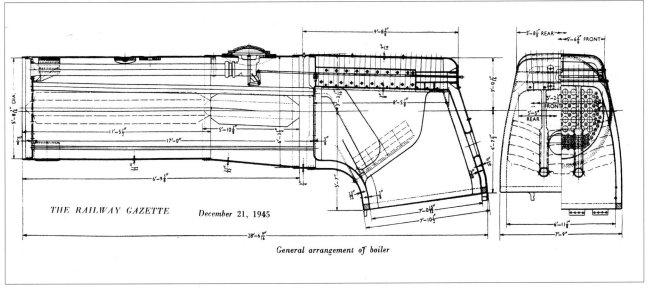

THE RAILWAY GAZETTE   December 21, 1945

General arrangement of boiler

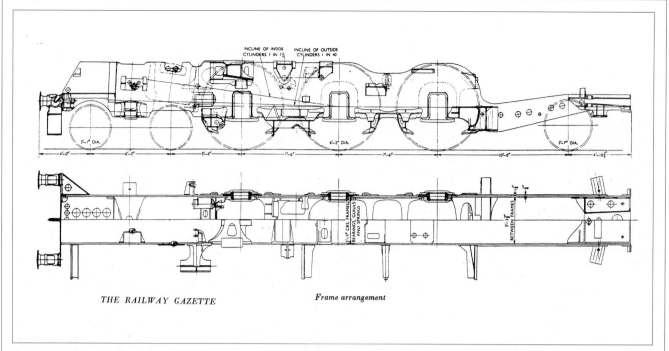

THE RAILWAY GAZETTE   Frame arrangement

Drawing right. **Bulleid found that his new wheels could not be heated up properly on existing equipment and instead of the tyre sitting stationary inside heating shoes it was revolved on a face plate inside stationary gas-fired heating shoes. These diagrams give some idea of the differences.**

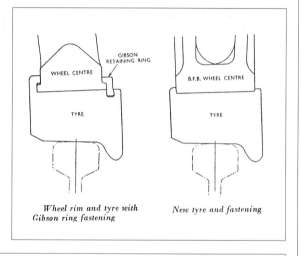

Wheel rim and tyre with Gibson ring fastening   *New tyre and fastening*

on 17 February 1941, running to Winchester and back the following day, A few days later it worked a ten coach test train to Bournemouth and back. None of this revealed any serious shortcomings it would appear and all was duly ready for its naming ceremony on 10 March 1941. Over the following weeks it worked on various trains but the *Southern Railway Magazine's* comments on its first official outing bearing the name ('it cut through the breeze with superlative ease') proved somewhat hyperbolic. Various faults manifested themselves, including the early embarrassment of the leaking tender tanks. War shortages meant that three sixteenth plate was used and this split when the water surged. The tender ran hot, too, and it was temporarily swapped with the one intended for 21C2, then being built – though this does not show on the record card.

The second Merchant, 21C2 UNION CASTLE, joined 21C1 at Salisbury shed, with the pair employed on heavy goods from there to Eastleigh and Exeter, the traffic having increased to such an extent 'as to demand greater power than was available hitherto'. The 'Packets' were taking heavy 800 ton goods over Honiton bank unaided but passenger traffic had not yet required the use of the new Pacifics. The cloak was coming off this 'general-service' business, however, and a trial was accordingly devised to demonstrate their ability to handle heavy express trains, a chance for which Bulleid was doubtless itching. Though the War was at its height, incredibly ROYAL MAIL with sixteen *empty* coaches left Waterloo briskly on 9 November 1941 easily attaining maximum permissible speeds everywhere. 21C2 UNION CASTLE took over at Salisbury and put up a similar show, cresting Honiton bank at over 25mph. It was a significant moment: *'This run amply demonstrated the ability of Mr O.V. Bulleid's new engines to handle any traffic likely to be assigned to them. Express trains of so great a weight have not hitherto been worked by one locomotive over the heavily-graded Salisbury-Exeter main line'.*

The rest of the 'first batch' of Merchant Navys followed through 1941 and the following year, ending with 21C10 BLUE STAR in July 1942.

THE RAILWAY GAZETTE   July 11, 1941

Internal and External Transport Link

The introduction of the second of the "Merchant Navy" class of locomotives, the *Union Castle*, which was named by Mr. Robertson F. Gibb at Victoria station on Friday, gave Mr. R. Holland-Martin an opportunity of saying what this new development of the Southern Railway meant in these days of war stress. He was explaining, by way of introducing Mr. Gibb, that some people wondered why his company should spend time on research and the manufacture and introduction of a new type of locomotive in war; but he believed that it was just in such times that every ounce of productive effort should be put forward. After all, as he suggested, Hitler was not abating any of the energies of his productive machines, so why should we? Probably what the Chairman of the Southern Railway Company had at the back of his mind was, not the use to which these new engines could be put in hauling the ocean expresses which cater for the vast Southampton passenger traffic, but their great advantage today when they can be turned to profitable employment as mixed traffic engines for hauling express goods trains whether for imperative war requirements or urgent civilian needs. Thus, again, the policy of long term research for the commerce of peace has been turned to the advantage of a national emergency. It was also a happy augury that—apart from the initial trial engine which, being the Southern Railway's own as it were, the *Channel Packet,* introduced the first of the commercial series—the *Union Castle* links up the railways with the merchant service just as Lord Leathers, who was represented on that occasion by Sir Cyril Hurcomb, has done in the newly co-ordinated Ministry of War Transport.

*   *   *   *

21C5 CANADIAN PACIFIC in March 1942 as built, in malachite with yellow stripes and, for reasons of good luck, or avoiding bad luck, the 'completed' horseshoe.

21C8 ORIENT LINE fresh out of works in wartime black in October 1942. Note *single* sanding hole, forward of nameplate, asbestos cloth over trailing truck (letting down somewhat the air-smoothed up-to-dateness of the design) and distorted far side footstep at the front – this last feature results from careless touching-up of the photograph!

The first of the third batch, 35021, under construction in 1948. The fabricated smokebox certainly had 'an irregular shape', as the BR Report into the proposed modification of the class pointed out, in January 1955. Note six washout plugs, clack valves, steam dome, whistle, boiler lagging and the sandbox openings, high up on the side above the lubrication pipe runs. Photograph Collection John Fry.

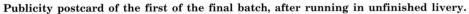

Publicity postcard of the first of the final batch, after running in unfinished livery.

The Curate's Egg

Losing Weight

The first two of the class turned out to be heavier than the Civil Engineer liked. This was of course often the case with new locomotives but the two Merchant Navys were too far over to be ignored – they weighed 99½ tons when they should have come out at 92½. Weight saving had to be embarked upon and until the matter was resolved the others of the ten, still in Eastleigh Works, could not be proceeded with. This was a serious situation, and could only be accomplished at great expense. The most rewarding target were the cast steel frame stretchers which could lose an eighth of an inch without deleterious effect, saving more than a ton in the process. Bulleid was stuck with the stretchers on the first two and could only have a further pattern of lightening holes drilled out, but the castings were refashioned for the next engines in the batch. Enlarging the lightening holes in the frames gained more, or rather less, weight and thinner plating was employed on the casing top, cab sides and smokebox. Lighter frames altogether were made for subsequent engines but the building of 21C3-21C5 was too advanced and these were modified by further holes being cut out.

The king-size number plates were retained on 21C1 and 21C2 until BR renumbering in 1949 and 1950 respectively. The plates for 21C3 had already been cast in fact, and could be found hanging about in Eastleigh Works for twenty years or more. The chimney cover and the top part of the casing around the chimney and in front of it was done away with which had the added advantage of further lifting the exhaust somewhat. It was even said that the wheel splashers under the casing were not fitted but as Winkworth (*Bulleid's Pacifics*) points out, at least one of the batch did in fact have the splashers. Perhaps the most extraordinary outcome (surely unique in British – maybe world – practice) was the resort to a non-metal board for the casing and cab. This 'limpet' board was a pressed asbestos fibre material and was used on the rest of the batch under construction, 21C3-21C10. The cab too was fashioned of the stuff (in all it saved some four tons) and the engines were easily distinguished by a prominent horizontal rib (often covered by the middle yellow line) along the 'waist' of the casing.

Smoke Deflectors 1

The air-smoothed casing was supposed to lift air, and with it the exhaust smoke, high and away from the cab but in this function, unfortunately, it failed. On 21C1 the casing was taken up above the level of the chimney rim with an 'air slot' in the smokebox front. It was between the top of the smokebox door and the 'widow's peak' of the casing, making a rectangular cut-out. Aerodynamics have a way of confounding expectations and the 'air slot' and the column of air it was supposed to force through, failed to lift the smoke. 21C2 under construction was accordingly altered with more of the area above the smokebox cut away and a square hole cut round the chimney. These changes were incorporated in the subsequent eight engines of 1941.

The Curate's Eggs

The 'Ten New Main Line Locomotives' the Southern now had were not proving an immediate success. They were largely used on freights because they were too unreliable for passenger work and the burden of maintenance and servicing was looking ominous. Bradley records that extra fitters had to be drafted in to Salisbury and Exmouth Junction. While work on say, a King Arthur might take an hour, comparable jobs on a Merchant Navy might demand double or treble that. It was as well that the men were available, from sheds in the Kentish Front Line largely closed down.

The engines were new and complicated, parts were sometimes difficult to get and staff and crews were often asked to do too much. Many small failures thus hit the engines' availability. On the road slipping was a problem but then again, this could (in part at least) be attributed to unfamiliarity of handling – as well as on-road oil leaks. There were not that many of the new engines and crews did

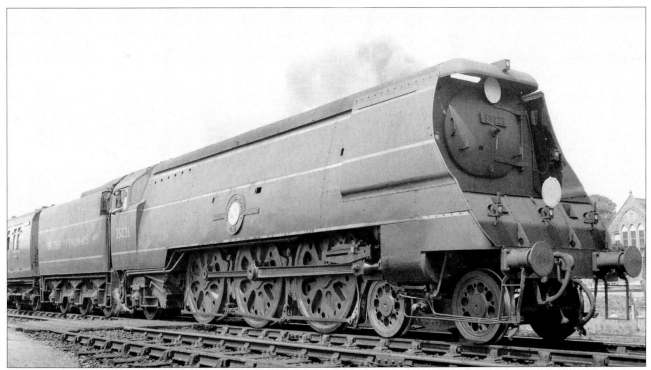

35023 HOLLAND-AFRIKA LINE, lettered BRITISH RAILWAYS and in its malachite green with horizontal yellow lines, at Templecombe about 1949. It went to Exmouth Junction shed and was there until 1960; accordingly it was a familiar engine on the Devon Belle – witness the batten on the smoke deflector for the side wing. Casing in front of cylinder later removed. Photograph W. Hermiston, The Transport Treasury.

Top left. The difference a curve makes. 21C10 BLUE STAR had been one of the 'mobile test beds' for smoke clearance trials in 1942-43 and had emerged from Eastleigh with a disastrous arrangement which included a shortened chimney. It was then that recourse was made to the men in white coats at Southampton and the 'cowl' later so familiar on all the Bulleid Pacifics came into being. BLUE STAR was thus the first to get the arrangement; here it is in black livery running into Basingstoke with a down West of England express. The short deflectors are 'flared out' from the casing and not 'bolted on', to use a somewhat laboured vocabulary. The point is, the sweep of the leading edge is as yet uninterrupted.

Bottom left. The difference a curve makes. BLUE STAR now has the 'standard' smoke deflectors fitted to the first ten over 1943-45; the break in curve at the front and the marked difference it makes to the appearance, can be readily appreciated. Photograph courtesy Hamish Stevenson.

were out of traffic rather too often, it is true, but matters did improve somewhat. By the autumn of 1943 the engines were regularly working expresses out of Waterloo and had entered on a high mileage pattern of passenger trains in-filled with fast freights. They were truly, like the Curate's Egg, 'good in parts', and getting better.

The changed situation had several reasons. Staff grew more adept at fixing things of course and growing familiarity all round meant conditions were less often allowed to become catastrophic. The infamous oil baths had been a thorn in the sheds' flesh from the beginning but little progress was made until a new pattern bath was fitted to 21C6 in 1944. This made for greatly reduced leakage but oil still

not get them day in day out. Coal consumption was also high, yet they steamed away 'fit to bust' with the worst wartime dross. They rode beautifully, the cab was a palace (though they were almost *too* comfy in hot weather while working hard) and they were powerful enough to run away with almost anything they were give. This was always the footplate crews' no.1 concern – for plenty of power they would forgive a lot. The new engines

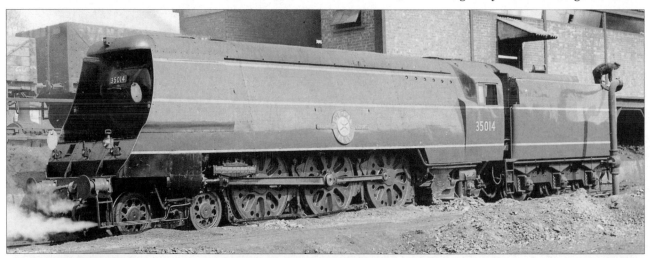

35014 NEDERLAND LINE in SR livery with BR number and smokebox plate. Smoke deflectors lengthened to extend to the rear of the cylinders, above the slidebar. The slidebar has one of the ill-fated covers, fitted to combat the sand that inevitably spilled from buckets. These had to be humped up a ladder but the job was not especially more difficult than on 'conventional' engines. It had always been a crude affair in Britain, loading sand but on an original Bulleid it was probably easier than most, in fact. You had to go up the footsteps for most engines, after all, and at least you were spared the hazards of an oily, slippery platform. 'Half' front faring painted black, something that was not common on a malachite green Merchant Navy; the tender is blank. NEDERLAND LINE is ex-works, on Eastleigh shed on 14 May 1949. Photograph J.H. Aston.

Above. NEDERLAND LINE in earlier manifestation, as 21C14 in malachite green with short deflectors, with trailing truck cover. This time it was not sand but ash that was the contaminant. Photograph Collection E.S. Youldon.

Left. Sand and sides on three separate engines. Note all the differences just in this small area of casing between 35004 CUNARD WHITE STAR, 35008 ORIENT LINE and 35010 BLUE STAR – and they were all from the same batch! That casing was always on and off and as anyone who has ever tried to get the panelling back on a car door knows, it never goes back *exactly* the same. Thus the wide range of edging, rivets, cuts, dents, patches and plates. BLUE STAR is the right-hand side, the other two the left-hand. Sanding was always a bugbear on the Merchant Navys, in which contamination from oil no doubt played a part. They had steam sanding but on the first ten it was only available to the front of the middle coupled wheels. The sand boxes were filled from these points high on the side, with the fireman clambering up a ladder. The inevitable spillage was the reason the slidebar covers were eventually tried out. On 21C1-21C10 the single sand hole was forward of the nameplate. Later, sanding had to be applied to all coupled wheels and a second sanding hole was made, as here to the rear of the plate, and a third for the front wheels even higher and close up by the smokebox. Sanding thereafter was to the front of each coupled wheel. The second batch and the final series had the same arrangement. Sanding on a Merchant Navy had to be planned a little like a military operation and it's not surprising that sand was liberally spilled. The sliding covers soon jammed and were usually left open but there was a further lid inside on the delivery pipe, a hinged cover which fell forward when opened to project through the sliding outer cover. One oddity was the rearward sanding to the leading tender wheel. Gravity sanding on the front of the tender prevented tender wheels from 'picking up' in poor adhesion conditions. 'Picking up' occurred when braking caused wheels to lock up and skid. This could happen when rails were wet and the tender relatively light, with coal and water low perhaps. One thing the arrangement was not, whatever has been written, was a method of sand delivery for rearward running. When rebuilt, the engines got three conventional sandboxes, overcoming the problem of tender first running by having delivery pipes to the front of the leading coupled wheel and to either side of the middle coupled wheel. All photographs J.L. Stevenson, courtesy Hamish Stevenson

got out and, worse, water still got in, causing corrosion. Bulleid called it 'continuous flood lubrication'; his idea was that, though the parts were inaccessible the reduced wear and freedom from heating meant that no attention would be needed between General repairs. In this he was wrong.

The practical difficulties of making a leak-proof bath enclosing three sets of valve motion as well as the middle connecting rod slide bar and crankpin, all inside the frames with the complication of relative movement, were immense. Two reversible gear

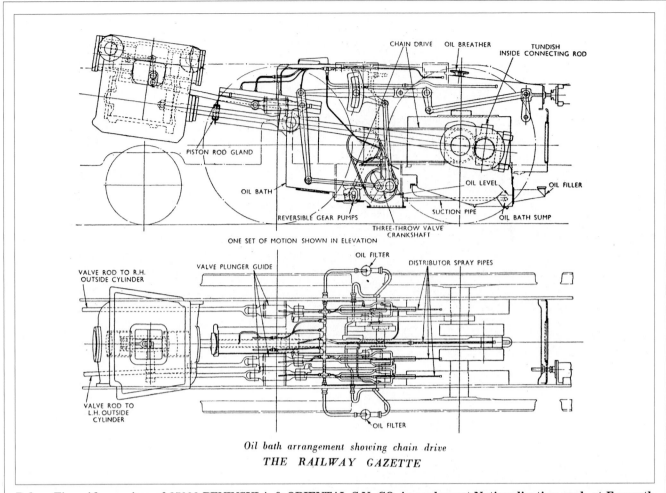

CHAIN DRIVE · OIL BREATHER · TUNDISH INSIDE CONNECTING ROD

PISTON ROD GLAND

OIL BATH

REVERSIBLE GEAR PUMPS

THREE-THROW VALVE CRANKSHAFT

ONE SET OF MOTION SHOWN IN ELEVATION

OIL LEVEL · OIL FILLER · OIL BATH SUMP · SUCTION PIPE

VALVE ROD TO R.H. OUTSIDE CYLINDER

VALVE PLUNGER GUIDE

OIL FILTER · DISTRIBUTOR SPRAY PIPES

VALVE ROD TO L.H. OUTSIDE CYLINDER

OIL FILTER

Oil bath arrangement showing chain drive
THE RAILWAY GAZETTE

Below. Fine side-on view of 35006 PENINSULA & ORIENTAL S.N. CO. in early post-Nationalisation garb at Exmouth Junction – shows the three sand filling holes to good effect. Note the loudspeaker on the pole. Tender is 3116, an original 5,000 gallon one with the high 'rave' and still with blackout slides on the front. Compare the curves of the casing at each end with the more angular style of the later batch – see the photograph of 35023 at Templecombe for instance. Photograph W. Hermiston, The Transport Treasury.

pumps chain driven from the valve crankshaft drew oil from the sump and forced it through discharging pipes over the moving parts. These tended to become clogged with bits of cleaning rag and so on but this too was overcome and in his paper to the Institution of Mechanical Engineers in December 1945, Bulleid claimed: 'Leakage of oil from the sump was considerable at first but this loss has been reduced, and the

consumption is now reasonable'. Special (expensive) emulsifying oil also had to be used. Bulleid also claimed that the chain drive 'behaved well' and that none had broken so far. Bradley, however, attributes the mishap and subsequent self-immolation experienced by 21C6 in December 1942 (near Honiton) to a chain parting. Six inch elongations in the chains were said to cause problems later but

Bulleid claimed to have more or less 'designed in' a three inch 'sag', and could see no problems in it.

Smoke Deflectors 2
Bulleid would have known of the Southampton University wind tunnel laboratory from his LNER days when P2 2-8-2's front end architecture was investigated there. The first modifications to the front ends, in 1941

Top. There was no better way of picking out the break of curve as the smoke deflectors met the sweep of the casing than to paint it white. This has conveniently been done for us on blue-liveried Royal engine 35019 FRENCH LINE CGT, working to Sherborne and passing Vauxhall on 1 June 1950. According to *The Railway Observer*, this was the visit of the King and Queen to Sherborne School, 'probably the longest non-stop ever recorded on Southern metals ... 118.2 miles between Waterloo and Sherborne'. Photograph K.G. Carr.

Above. The short deflectors still on 21C12 UNITED STATES LINE, the first Southern engine to get a coat of malachite green, near the end of the War in April 1945. It still has the original cab, and two side windows. Photograph Collection E.S. Youldon.

(*Smoke Deflectors 1*) had involved some brief tests with a 1:10 model. These 1941 modifications were not a lasting solution, however, and complaints had continued – 21C6, 21C7 and 21C10 for instance got experimental and apparently valueless deflectors for a while in 1943. So, after drawing up various solutions (reminiscent of A4s and the P2 COCK O' THE NORTH) which never materialised, in 1942-43 Bulleid turned again to the boffins at Southampton. More or less conventional smoke deflectors were found to be the answer but the great departure, which came to characterise the Merchant Navys and the light Pacifics after them, was the making of a cowl, brought forward beyond the smokebox front, to augment the deflectors. The proper lab-approved plates with cowl were applied thus:

21C1	12/43
21C2	6/44
21C3	9/44
21C4	1/44
21C5	3/44
21C6	4/44
21C7	8/44
21C8	6/43
21C9	6/43
21C10	4/43

Cabs 1

The Merchant Navys involved a lot of extra work in their operation and maintenance, not least at the sheds. It was ironic, therefore, that labour *saving* was paramount in the designer's mind. The casing too, had labour saving, if not at its heart, then at least it was in the equation, for Bulleid intended (so it is said) that his Pacifics should be able to run through carriage washing plants – no cleaning gangs needed! This was one reason why the first cabs followed the profile of the

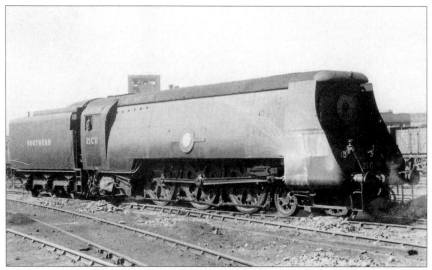

The horrible bulbous front end faring (priming salts forced through the seams and looking generally awful) as applied to 21C11 GENERAL STEAM NAVIGATION. It had mercifully been cut back by half (by 1948) and then disappeared entirely. Cover prominent on trailing truck.

casing so intimately. They were streets ahead of anything else in comfort, except that at times in summer when the fireman was hard at it they could feel over-warm. Ultra violet lamps provided a glimmer for certain controls during night-time.

Cabs 2

Cabs on the second batch were similar in appearance though the curve and the window edge at the front was slightly different, the layout of rivets varied and back sheets were provided to make the seats either side cosier, shielding them from cross draughts. Yet the sliver of cab front that was possible within the loading profile was just that, a sliver, and the space available for the window was desperately small. The outlook from the cab, or rather lack of it, was accordingly a perennial cause of complaint. To give a broader window

within the profile a 'wedge' or 'V' cab provided an answer; these were appearing on some light Pacifics in August 1947 so one was put on a Merchant Navy, 21C8 ORIENT LINE at the same time – it was unique, in a 'V' shape, and led the way to the final style. It was this type of cab, with three side windows, that afterwards became familiar on all the Bulleid Pacifics. The third batch, 35021-35030, got these cabs from new. The dates are as follows, taken from Winkworth's *Bulleid's Pacifics* (21C8 had got two windows at first; three were provided from 7/49):

21C1-35001	12/50
21C2-35002	1/54
21C3-35003	5/50
21C4-35004	10/50
21C5-35005	2/50
21C6-35006	3/51
21C7-35007	3/50
21C8-35008	8/47

21C2 with its cowl and smoke deflector arrangement, climbing Honiton bank. Very dirty post-war condition, with faded malachite and stripes and gunmetal plates still on front, cab and tender. In fact it kept the metal plates until January 1950 by which time its livery was truly deplorable. Eastleigh was touchingly reluctant to dispose of the plates – the engine even survived a works visit in September 1949 without getting renumbered! Photograph W. Hermiston, The Transport Treasury.

21C9-35009	2/53
21C10-35010	11/49
21C11-35011	9/50
21C12-35012	3/49
21C13-35013	12/52
21C14-35014	5/49
21C15-35015	6/49
21C16-35016	6/49
21C17-35017	4/48
21C18-35018	5/48
21C19-35019	4/48
21C20-35020	5/48

That futuristic cab. A black garbed 21C6 shows the cabside at close quarters to be a panoply of rivet work. Note the rather embarrassing cover over the trailing axlebox. Photograph The Transport Treasury.

Windows

The Merchant Navys, of course, couldn't even have the same windows. Put briefly, the first two and the last ten had gun metal frames, the other eighteen had wooden ones. There was nearly uniformity in the number of windows, however – all had three apart from one exception (naturally) which had only two. This was 21C8 – and the feature is clear in photographs taken before July 1949.

Valancing

Associated with changes in the curvature of the fronts, the smoke deflectors and so on, and the general passage of time, the curved (at times distinctly bulbous) valancing between the front of the cylinders and the buffer beam gradually disappeared, for much the same reason as on the LNER A4s. They didn't really do much and were a nuisance to get off when work had to be done. This area, between the front of the cylinders and the buffer beam, was fully enclosed on the first one and more or less enclosed on the subsequent

Smoke deflectors taken to the limit. These uniquely lengthy plates, fitted (to 35020 only) in 1948 in connection with the forthcoming Exchange Trials, certainly lifted smoke even more effectively than previous plates, but they obstructed forward vision, and were not proceeded with on other Merchant Navys. They covered up, of course, the forward sander and though a sliding hatch was made in the plates themselves, these were eventually abandoned as too awkward and were simply removed and the access plated over so they could not be used again. The position can just be discerned by that rectangular outline in this photograph. BIBBY LINE (at Nine Elms in July 1953) was the only Merchant Navy so fitted and kept them until rebuilding. The tender was modified as shown after the Crewkerne accident. Cab lining has been modified to suit the panelled tender. Photograph The Transport Treasury.

nine of the first batch. The second batch were somewhat similar except for 21C11 which was a kind of throwback, cursed with a hideously bulbous arrangement which looked like an early experiment in fibre glass moulding gone wrong. The third batch were somewhat similar to the previous engines, 21C12-21C20. With some 'local variation' the valance migrated upwards, with a trend to disappearance, over time. Their good looks suffered because of it.

Ten More – The Second Batch

Whatever the problems, the sheds were getting on top of them by 1944 and it was clear that when working well, the Merchant Navys were capable of anything. The order for ten more boilers, additional to the original ten had been in at North British since 1940 but by now the new machinery was installed at Eastleigh (see the previous section) so that production could be done there instead of Glasgow. There were some difficulties at first, for some of the techniques were new but 21C11, the first of the second batch, was ready at the very end of 1944, on 31 December that year. Thinner frames than those on 21C1-21C10 were used, to lessen weight, along with a thinner (this time

Left. **The first twenty Merchant Navys had this cast steel form of trailing truck, covered at first by asbestos cloth (some say canvas or leather, some Rexene!) sheeting which was generally abandoned as useless after the War. Ash, ominously, is trickling onto the main casting... The oval plate is the mud hole door cover. Photograph Collection Alec Swain, The Transport Treasury.**

GENERAL STEAM NAVIGATION in black at Nine Elms in 1946. Note one-piece crosshead and piston rod; later this was developed into two separate, cottered components. Mechanical linkage for drain cocks is clear to see, along with the bulbous extra casing ahead of the cylinders. Note front sand pipes. Photograph Collection Alec Swain, The Transport Treasury.

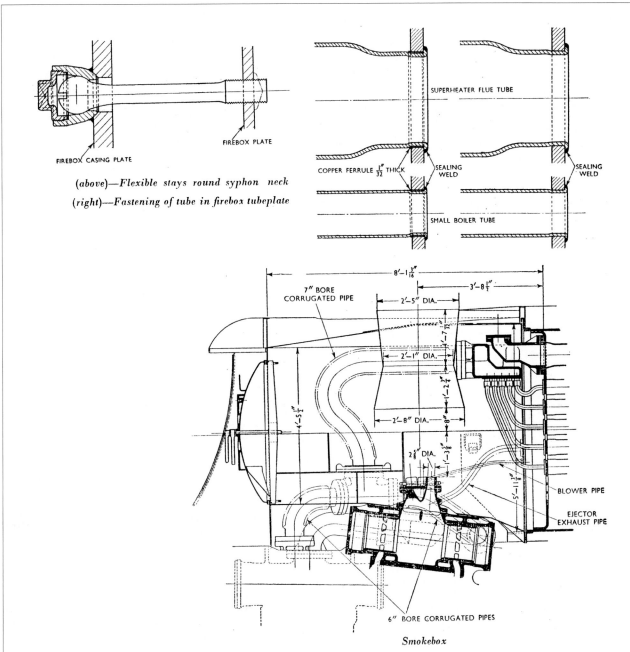

FIREBOX CASING PLATE

FIREBOX PLATE

SUPERHEATER FLUE TUBE

COPPER FERRULE $\frac{1}{32}$" THICK

SEALING WELD

SEALING WELD

SMALL BOILER TUBE

(above)—*Flexible stays round syphon neck*
(right)—*Fastening of tube in firebox tubeplate*

8'-1$\frac{3}{16}$"

7" BORE CORRUGATED PIPE

2'-5" DIA.

3'-8$\frac{1}{2}$"

2'-1" DIA.

2'-8" DIA.

4'-5$\frac{1}{2}$"

2$\frac{5}{8}$" DIA.

BLOWER PIPE

EJECTOR EXHAUST PIPE

6" BORE CORRUGATED PIPES

Smokebox

Drawings, from *The Railway Gazette* of 28 December 1945 (taken in turn from Bulleid's paper to the Institution of Mechanical Engineers a fortnight or so before) to show stay and tube details and the smokebox configuration by that time. The smokebox diagram is of interest in showing the new corrugated (and thereby flexible) steampipes adopted by now. Originally they had been cast but were prone to cracking; this new arrangement solved the problem.

metal – the 'limpet' board could be devastated by the slightest shed yard collision) casing. Further weight was saved by altering the disposition of the boiler barrel; this time the front ring was parallel where before it had been tapered. The taper from now on was taken up on the rear ring, at the bottom – see the first section, *Ten New Main Line Locomotives*.

Smoke Deflectors 3
The second ten engines, 21C11-21C20 had the cowl and smoke deflectors which had been so painfully arrived at for the first ten, though naturally they varied somewhat. The first ten 'swept out' from the casing as it were leaving the leading edge of the casing uninterrupted. On the second ten the

plates were more obviously bolted on, as distinct attachments and from the front this was evident from the break of curve. The deflector plates on 21C11-21C20 were short at first, extending no farther back than the rear of the cylinders.

The Last Ten – The Third and Final 'BR' Batch
The concentration of work at Eastleigh, which had occurred for the building of the second batch was now reversed, due to the post-war dislocation of staff and equipment. The cylinders and frames were to be built at Ashford, boilers and tenders at Brighton and the rest of the bits provided by Eastleigh, which would assemble the locomotives. The orders were put in place in 1947, before

Nationalisation, but the first engine was not ready for a year or more, such were the difficulties with materials and parts. So it was that the last ten bore BR numbers from the first, 35021 to 35030, going out from September 1948 to April 1949.

Smoke Deflectors 4
The final development of smoke deflectors on the original Merchant Navys was a larger type, extending back beyond the rear of the cylinders, giving a better balance to the whole locomotive. The curious super-elongation of the plates on 35020 BIBBY LINE* aside, the existing twenty locos got these better proportioned 'bolted on' plates within a year or two. 21C1-21C10 got them in

place of their 'flared' ones as they went through works down to 1945 and the second batch 21C11-21C20 got them in place of their 'short' plates as they went into works in due course after delivery in 1944-45. The final, 'BR' batch 35021-35030 of 1948-49 had the longer smoke deflectors from new; it was this final version that came to characterise the class until they were rebuilt.

35020 BIBBY LINE was standby engine for the 1948 trials, and the long deflectors were related to its possible 'foreign' employment, although 35017 and 35019 on the trials retained normal deflectors. The light Pacifics that went far and wide (34004, 34005 and 34006) were, however, all given long deflectors.

Mechanical Stoker

Bulleid wanted to try out a mechanical stoker on one of the Merchant Navys almost from the first, announcing in *The Railway Gazette* that 'adequate steam raising in a locomotive boiler under all conditions can be assured *only* [my emphasis] by fitting a mechanical stoker'. War conditions prevented him acquiring the necessary equipment and it was not until October 1947 that the Southern Railway took delivery of a reconditioned Berkley mechanical stoker – the firm was the one that later provided stokers for the BR 9Fs. 'It was not one of the best-known American stokers' writes Reed in the *Loco Profile* 'but it happened to have a representative in England'.

It was March 1948 before it could be fitted, to 21C5 (S prefix added the same month and renumbered 35005 the next month) at Eastleigh Works. The equipment involved minor rearrangements on the tender for a coal pusher; this got the coal forward to the screw and up to a distributor plate. From here was put about the firebox by steam jets. Coal of a fairly uniform size was necessary and the front of the screw was effectively a coal crusher. One is inclined to suspect that the dust and effort, curses and sometimes danger associated with the thing, together with its 'new-fangled' character (crews after all only came into contact with it intermittently) probably doomed it whatever happened. Before that, a surprisingly extensive series of trials were made from Eastleigh shed, conveniently close to the works. It certainly sounded more or less perfect when described in the press: '*A particular advantage of the stoker is that it can adequately deal with varying types of fuel; it crushes the coal, without producing an undesirable amount of dust, to a size easily dispersed by the steam jets over the whole length and width of the grate. It is capable of handling slack coal in wet or dry condition, as well as the hardest run of mine coal*'.

After some further works attention 35005 went to Nine Elms, running nearly 60,000 miles with the mechanical stoker before finding itself back at Eastleigh for a Heavy Intermediate. It then went to Rugby for evaluation on the Testing Plant, running road trips on the LMR with the mobile test unit. This was also taken on to the Southern, running trips between Stewarts Lane and Salisbury. These tests finished on 4 April 1950.

The stoker was taken out at Eastleigh to compare conditions with the engine fired conventionally – *Trains Illustrated* of July 1950 pointing out that it might be more appreciated on an LMR or the ER Garratt where 'its robot activity would be vastly appreciated by the engine crews'. The SR would not give up and after further modification the stoker was installed yet again on 35005, in June 1950. Once again 35005 worked from Nine Elms, mainly on the Bournemouth line but a more than usually destructive chain gear failure three months later saw it hauled back dead to Eastleigh, in October 1950. Undeterred, the SR added LMR-style self cleaning equipment in the smokebox and prepared the engine for yet more stoker trials. These finally petered out in April 1951, 35005 having run 77,738 miles with the stoker in place. Apart from the vast quantities of coal burnt and the inordinate volumes of smoke belched out nothing about the episode was especially notable. Leaving Eastleigh on 27 April 1951 35005 was at last free of the equipment and returned to Exmouth Junction. The tender (3115) was converted back to the standard first series form though when 35005 was rebuilt in May 1959 it was rebodied with a 5,250 gallon tank.

Top left and above. On the last series, for reasons of weight saving, this fabricated version of the cast trailing truck was substituted. Subsequently these were mixed willy-nilly at Eastleigh, the early cast versions appearing randomly on 35021-35030, and the later fabricated ones on the earlier twenty, 35001-35020. The ashpan was in three sections, one between the frames, the other two outside; note the dampers either side, fitted from new on the third series and opened from the cab, on 35025 BROCKLEBANK LINE, at Nine Elms in 1952. At the bottom of the ashpan is the curved 'self cleaning' hopper door operated from rail level, using a handle a bit like a hefty broomstick – accidents sometimes occurred resulting in this door welding itself to the third rail! 'Small additional cleaning doors at the back' (according to Bulleid's paper to the Institution of Mechanical Engineers in 1946) 'enabled any ash accumulation at the rear to be dislodged'. That's the dynamo behind the trailing truck under the cab rear, a 24V Stone's generator. Photograph Collection Alec Swain, The Transport Treasury.

Below. Study in injectors on BROCKLEBANK LINE, Nine Elms, 1952. Note linkages to injector controls in the cab. The two feed pipes run from the injectors forward and under the casing to the clack valves. On the rebuilt engines of course, these pipe runs and the clacks were visible at their extremities, though they remained hidden by the footplating in between. Photograph Collection Alec Swain, The Transport Treasury.

35019 FRENCH LINE CGT with LMS tender 10219 sweeps past the Great Western engine shed at Reading with an up test train from the west of England on one of the Plymouth workings at the end of April 1948, GW dynamometer car in tow. The SR engines involved in the trials got Flaman speed recorders – indicated by the bracket by the rear driving wheel.

Testing Times

Locomotive Exchanges 1948

These Exchanges have been exhaustively 'gone over' down through the years but, hoping not to repeat too much, they remain very much part of the Merchant Navy story. Their purpose was to determine 'the most desirable features to incorporate in the design of future steam locomotives' though it is doubtful whether the times and place of the trials could ever really have provided for this. Ordinary service trains on lines often badly affected by post-war deficiencies, driven to no discernible common pattern hardly provided incontestable data.

The steam locomotives used came direct from traffic, normally having run between 15-20,000 miles since their last General Repair and besides this 'on the road' testing it was intended that they should be run at the Swindon and Rugby Testing Plants too – which took some years and became increasingly irrelevant as the BR Standard series was established.

The Merchant Navys involved in the trials were 35017, 35018 and 35019 with 35020 as a spare engine, running on test (there was a week's preliminary running before each week of tests) with dynamometer car as follows:-

35019 on the 1.30pm Paddington-Plymouth North Road on 27 and 29 April; balanced workings were the 8.30am Plymouth North Road-Paddington, 28 and 30. 35017 on the 1.10pm Kings Cross-Leeds on 25 and 27 May; balanced workings were the 7.50am Leeds-Kings Cross on 26 and 28 May. This engine also worked the 10am Euston-Carlisle on 11 and 13 May; balanced workings were the 12.55pm Carlisle-Euston on 12 and 14 May.

35018 was used on its home Region, on the 10.50am Waterloo-Exeter Central on 1 and 3 June; balanced workings were the 12.37pm Exeter Central to Waterloo on 2 and 4 June – both trains, in fact, were the 'Atlantic Coast Express'.

Predictably, at several times with good rail conditions, partial slipping for considerable distances was recorded with the Merchant Navys and, in one instance with a light Pacific. 35019 in one incident slipped for 2¼ miles on Rattery Bank between Totnes and Wrangaton in Devon. They worked with somewhat different cut-offs and so on while on the various main lines and, characteristically, steamed freely and well. On the Paddington-Plymouth run for instance 35019 ran

away with itself, the safety valves lifting on Hemerdon Bank at 270lb. And of course they rode well, as would be expected.

There were minor faults experienced, of precisely the niggling type which kept their availability low at home on the Southern. On 27 April 35019 had three fusible plugs leaking at the threads at Plymouth and on 28 April firebox stays below the firehole door were blowing badly. On 25 May 35017 had to have attention to the non-return valves; the cylinder lubrication was 'playing up' and (an old one this) the steam reversing gear was causing trouble, owing to the cut-off position not being held.

The SR crews could hardly expect to be expert in the use of water scoops (but what was the Inspector doing?) and on 11 May the pick up gear on the LMR tender attached to 35017 took a whack, which meant an extra water stop at Lancaster. Two days later, after the Euston-Carlisle run, four stays were found leaking in the firebox, two of them blowing badly and repairs were effected. There were other minor ailments, particularly to do with lubrication and, however much the Exchange Trials fell short of a stern analysis upon which to build a

35019 FRENCH LINE CGT at Wakefield on a pre-test run (no dynamometer car, note). It worked on Whit Monday 17 May 1948 and returned from Leeds the next day, failing, according to *The Railway Observer* 'with a blowhole in a thermic syphon'.

35017 BELGIAN MARINE heads up Holloway Bank on test in the Exchange Trials – destination Leeds. Cecil J. Allen wrote of one climb with the SR engine from Grantham to Stoke Summit in *The Locomotive Exchanges 1870-1948* (Ian Allan 1949) declaring that he could not find any record of a start with a comparably loaded LNER Pacific 'quite as fast as this'. Photograph Collection E.S. Youldon.

Standard fleet, they did, almost perfectly, show up the strengths and weaknesses of the Merchant Navy design. Strong, free steaming, beautifully riding and at times brilliant engines, brought low by too many elementary defects and a high coal/water consumption.

The Southern engines (the Merchant Navys and the light Pacifics) in fact did rather better than the framework of the Exchange Trials allowed. Winkworth (*Bulleid's Pacifics*) makes the telling point for instance, that the SR engines were among the best in keeping to the timetables, which is arguably a more desirable state of affairs (for the passenger) than arriving twenty minutes late having saved a bit of coal on the way. The Southern engines seemed to have been run 'flat out' to give good times and high power outputs, and coal and water per mile would necessarily have been on the high side; moreover, SR engines figured in the highest power output figures out of all proportion to their numbers. Other Pacifics were quite capable of reaching these levels and the significance of the figures is their indication of differing ways of driving. If the others had ran 'flat out' the consumption figures might have been more comparable.

35019 FRENCH LINE CGT shows its paces with the Western Region dynamometer car at Bruton, the gangers more taken with the cameraman than this other stranger in their midst. Photograph Collection E.S. Youldon.

BIBBY LINE was the spare for the Locomotive Exchanges and though it stayed at home had to be fitted out for work in the event of failure among the other three. It thus ran like this on the Southern (this is Southampton Central) equipped with speed recorder and Stanier tender. In the event it was not needed.

BR Performance and Efficiency Tests - March 1952-January 1954

No one was really happy with the outcome of the 1948 Exchanges and in the ensuing years the availability of the new Rugby Test Plant meant that a more studied and objective appreciation could be made of the capabilities of the various types. The value of all this work had to be doubted at least slightly, given that by now the future course of the BR Standard fleet was more or less set. However, 35022 HOLLAND-AMERICA LINE was selected for a number of tests, both stationary and on the road, which took place between March 1952 and January 1954; the results were published in British Transport Commission British Railways Bulletin No.10, *Performance & Efficiency Tests of Southern Region 'Merchant Navy' class 3 cylinder 4-6-2 mixed traffic locomotive*. The Bulletin was prepared by the Rugby and Derby testing staff and was published in January 1954 at the splendid price of ten shillings. HOLLAND-AMERICA LINE was a high mileage loco which was unusual for this programme of tests. Maybe the SR thought the results would have no tangible effect whatever the outcome and pragmatism dictated that an engine was sent that would be missed least; re-building, even scrapping was in the air and maybe it was not in the Region's interest for the engine to do well at all... The Test Bulletin put it another way: 'The engine was prepared for testing during a classified repair and ran 1,115 miles in traffic before commencement of the tests. During the first series of plant tests it ran 10,300 miles and 3,840 miles on the road'.

35022 HOLLAND AMERICA LINE, the engine which spent so much time on Rugby Test Plant and taking 'the largest number of bogie coaches ever operated' over the Skipton-Carlisle route, on home ground on Honiton bank. Photograph W. Hermiston, The Transport Treasury.

BIBBY LINE, of course, more than made up for the anonymity of the Locomotive Exchanges by fracturing its axle at Crewkerne, as these familiar pictures *(above and below right)* record. Quite what left the engine (it was doing 70-80mph) to half demolish the canopy of Crewkerne station does not seem to be recorded, though it was almost certainly chunks of brake gear, and this was the scene afterwards. To this day, the steel uprights that replaced the demolished cast iron round columns can be identified. It was the felling of the columns that brought the roof down. The centre driving wheel, leaning drunkenly when the loco came to rest, had been held more or less in line by the motion which, though it buckled and bent, thankfully held at the last.

There were three main elements to the testing, all using 35022 HOLLAND-AMERICA LINE:

- the first (main) set, running the locomotive 'on the rollers' and out on the road between March and October-November 1952;

- a second set examining a configuration of single blastpipe, on the SR and

- a third set running the engine with a firebox without thermic syphons.

First Set of Tests – Rugby Stationary Plant and on the Road

The first part of the tests, on the plant rollers, took place from March 1952 with the engine deemed to be in its 'as designed' state. Tests, it was hoped, would 'define the relationship between coal as fired and water as drawn from the tender, tractive effort and horsepower, both as available at the tender drawbar'. This saw the use of three different coals – South Kirkby, a grade 1A hard coal from South Yorkshire, Blidworth, a grade 2B hard from the East Midlands and Bedwas, a grade 2A soft coal from South Wales. This last was friable with a lot of dust and regarded as more closely similar to that normally used for the Bulleid Pacifics.

Working of the locomotive was in two distinctive ways:

1) with relatively short cut-offs and fully or nearly fully open regulator and 2) at relatively long cut-off and partially open regulator.

The Merchant Navy was not going to give up its secrets easily; the locomotive proved difficult to test owing to inconsistent performances and it was thus impossible to obtain reasonable accuracy or repetition on different occasions, for performance would sometimes change appreciably over quite short periods of time. 'Accurate measurement was exceptionally difficult, especially on the stationary test plant'. 'Phenomena of a kind known to be characteristic of this class' were found which 'may vary from one engine to another and from time to time'. The reason was the valve gear and its unfathomable behaviour inside that bath.

Cut-off relationships could not be definitely established for reversing gear and cylinders and results were downgraded to 'general representations'. On one day tests made a recorded pull at 15mph that was double that of the day before and at 20mph more than half as large again! The cut-off changed apparently of its own volition and in some cases the indicated cut-off could not be relied upon to be correct, for power outputs that were theoretically impossible for

particular cut-offs were recorded. The steam reversing gear 'crept' slightly when the engine was working so special 'distance' pieces were made to hold it in a definite fixed position. These of course could only be changed when the engine was stopped on the rollers. Slipping was alarming. The old bugbear, leaking lubrication oil, reached the wheel treads and the Test Plant Rollers had to be wiped at regular intervals. It even led 'to buckling coupling rods which happened a number of times in the stationary plant and on the line.' In the confines of the Test Plant, this must have been truly terrifying. Steps, it was noted, 'were already in hand to redesign the … coupling rods'. At the stationary plant the period of the tests varied between 60 and 150 minutes and there were a number of shorter ones on the determination of power outputs and steaming rates only. Failures on the Test Plant included heated coupled axleboxes, heating of inside big ends, heated coupling rod bushes and so on. It was damage to the rollers themselves, however, and the catastrophic consequences that might flow from such an unwelcome event, that was uppermost in the testers' minds. Fearing for their lives they shrank, understandably, from pursuing 35022's maximum boiler capacity. Maximum steaming rates on the plant were found to be 33,300lb/hr with Blidworth, 37,000lb/hr with Bedwas and (briefly) a peak of 42,000lb/hr with South Kirkby (this would be true 'collar work').

The Controlled Road Testing that followed took place over the Skipton-Carlisle route October-November 1952 and there was, inevitably 'some discrepancy between the results of the plant tests and those on the line'. On the line the duration of the journeys were between 65 to 75 minutes though some were shorter. Sustained rates of firing of over 3,000lb/hr were attained, employing two firemen 'to avoid undue fatigue'. This sort of rate was greater than anything normally required from the Merchant Navys.

Out on the road the 'Swindon Type Steam Flow Indicator' was used and the ranges of speed, nominal cut-off and steaming rate were all appreciably less in the 'real world' than on the stationary plant: *'The maximum steaming rate was limited to about 29,000lb/hr, which sufficed to work a train of 20 bogie coaches of 594 tons at the scheduled speed involved ... [this was] the largest number of bogie coaches ever operated over this route'*. On line slipping was again the great shortcoming, the engine experiencing buckled coupling rods.

On conclusion of the first set of investigations the Test Committee felt

that 'as designed' the Merchant Navy was *'a most effective and capable engine but one that is relatively uneconomical. If operating, as they frequently are in service, with the reversing gear in a relatively long cut-off and with the regulator very little opened [they] will be still less economical though their performance will then be more reliable from the mechanical point of view and from that of power output'* Combustion was 'never very good, especially with the lower grade coal'.

Some improvement suggested were:-
Wider spacing of the grate bars.
Provision of a deflector plate.
Admission of more air through the firehole door with the doors closed.
New chimney design – *see next set of tests.*

Second Set of Tests – Modified Chimney with Single Blastpipe

All the Merchant Navys were built with a single large diameter chimney employing multiple jet blastpipes and the 'new chimney design' involved a smaller diameter one with a single blastpipe. As it happened, the Merchant Navy chimney had been occupying minds on the Southern for a year or more and 35019 FRENCH LINE C.G.T. had been so equipped in June 1951. It reacted indifferently despite alterations running into the following year, 1952. Time was lost, crews complained and the multiple

blastpipe went back on in September 1954. Despite this, the Rugby test engine, 35022 HOLLAND-AMERICA LINE was also fitted with single blastpipe, in February 1953 but results do not appear to have been much different than with FRENCH LINE C.G.T.. It was run on the Test Plant again during March-May 1953. With the modified chimney it ran 2,460 miles at the test plant and then returned to traffic.

The essence of the problem was the height available between the top of the inside valve chest and the top of the chimney, with the latter of course dictated by the loading gauge. The main reasons for the 'high' position of the inside steam chest were:

a) the inclination of the inside cylinder in order for the connecting rod to clear the leading coupled axle and

b) the position of the inside steamchest directly above its cylinder.

The distance to the top of the chimney was very restricted for so large a locomotive and a larger blastpipe was desirable to direct the exhaust better. (Remember how the design had been shoe-horned with marvellous skill into the restrictive Eastern Section profile.) None of the combinations of blast pipe and chimney gave results up to the standard set by the multiple jet

arrangement normally fitted to the class: *'use of the multiple jet arrangement is practically unavoidable if anything like full use is to be made of the steaming capacity of the boiler when inferior coal is used'*. The work ended in May 1953.

Third Set of Tests – Boiler without Thermic Syphons

The jury had long been 'out' on the efficacy of thermic syphons in British conditions, where boilers were relatively small. The fourth and final element of the test series therefore examined an engine without this equipment. The boiler, No.1107, had been fitted with a non-thermic syphon firebox more than a year before and was running on 35014 NEDERLAND LINE. Steaming had not been as good, despite alterations to the brick arch, though it was deemed satisfactory by the spring of 1952. The boiler and firebox were afterwards put on to 35022 HOLLAND-AMERICA LINE and after running in it duly made its way back to Rugby in December 1953, returning in the January of the following year.

Without thermic syphons 35022 ran 2,820 miles on the stationary test plant. Despite the full panoply of modern test equipment there was little that could usefully be said and the Test Committee could never really be sure whether such differences as were discerned were due to the absence of thermic syphons or the rearranged brick arch: 'such differences as were observed may have been due to as much to the different arch as to the absence of the syphons.' Other imponderables concerned the quality of the coal ('it left something to be desired resulting in bad clinkering of the grate and 'birdnesting' of the tubeplate') 35022 was more difficult to fire correctly than on the previous test and combustion was not improved nor was smoke emission reduced. 'Removal of the thermic syphons had virtually no effect on the maximum output of the boiler' though their removal and a different brick arch saw an increase in the inlet steam temperature of some 40 to 60 degrees Fahrenheit. It was not worthwhile, concluded the Report, 'on boiler performance grounds alone', to remove the thermic syphons; moreover it was not worthwhile to fit them in any British coal-fired locomotive of similar or smaller size especially if hand firing was required. 'An advantage' would be expected, however, in improved steam consumption from the higher superheat resulting from the removal of the syphons.

This was all becoming increasingly academic of course, for re-building – or even scrapping – of the class was now very much in the air.

BIBBY LINE and the Axle Emergency

On 24 April 1953 35020 BIBBY LINE, working the 2.15pm Plymouth-Waterloo train, suffered a broken middle driving axle, approaching Crewkerne at an estimated speed of 70-80mph. The crank axle fractured through 'the sprocket seating of the left-hand axle piece'.

35020 had run 353,256 miles since it was new in July 1947, 154,322 miles since its last General Repair in May 1950 and 49,273 miles since its last Intermediate in June 1952. The offending crank axle was No.E4237, manufactured at Eastleigh to Drawing No.E31968, and had run with the locomotive all its life. Crank axle pieces had been made from steel to Southern Railway specification No.324; they were normally visually examined at shop repairs and the crank pins tested magnetically.

On 27 April 1953, a week after the mishap, instructions were sent out for magnetic crack detection test to be carried out on all crank axles on all the Bulleid Pacifics.

Practical investigation using supersonic flaw detector equipment commenced at Eastleigh on 10 May and the very next day, 11 May instructions went out that all Merchant Navys would be withdrawn from service 'that night' until all crank axles had been tested on a magnetic flaw detector at Eastleigh. The work was complete on all but two of the class by 18 May; 35022 HOLLAND-AMERICA LINE was still on its interminable tests at the Rugby plant and would be examined in due course.

Flaws were found in the sprocket seating of crank axles on fourteen Merchant Navys; the other fourteen were returned to traffic. However, during the stripping down of one of the faulty crank axles (in order to investigate the problem further) more damage was detected, in the axle pieces under the web seats. It was then decided that the fourteen 'returnees' should be further tested by the ultrasonic flaw detector. The fourteen that *were* showing flaws on the sprocket seating should be completely stripped down and examined for flaws on the axle pieces under the webs. As a result nineteen crank axles (and their engines of course) had to be withdrawn from service – 35022 turned out to free of the affliction – either from flaws in the sprocket seating (14) or in the crank web seats (5).

Merchant Navy Class Locomotives.

Locomotive No.	Crank Axle No.	Mileage of Crank Axle at date of examination.	Motive Power Depot	Initial reason for locomotive being withdrawn from Traffic		Result of subsequent examination of crank axle when stripped		
				Sprocket Seat (Magnetic Test)	Web Seat (Supersonic Test)	Sprocket Seat (R.H. axle piece)	Web Seat L.H.	R.H.
35001	4072	524,794	Exmouth Junction	–	flawed	clear	flawed	flawed
35005	4090	383,729	Exmouth Junction	flawed	✱	flawed	flawed	flawed
35007	4063	393,130	Salisbury	flawed	✱	flawed	flawed	flawed
35008	4117	545,057	Salisbury	flawed	✱	flawed	flawed	flawed
35009	4642	278,222	Salisbury	flawed	✱	flawed	flawed	clear
35011	4156	372,659	Nine Elms	flawed	✱	flawed	flawed	flawed
35012	5233	208,927	Nine Elms	–	flawed	clear	flawed	flawed
35013	4201	369,124	Nine Elms	flawed	✱	flawed	flawed	flawed
35014	4108	432,393	Nine Elms	flawed	✱	flawed	flawed	flawed
35015	4192	379,797	Nine Elms	–	flawed	clear	flawed	flawed
35017	4210	389,273	Nine Elms	flawed	✱	flawed	flawed	flawed
35018	3848	188,201	Nine Elms	–	flawed	clear	flawed	clear
35019	4228	247,678	Nine Elms	flawed	✱	flawed	flawed	flawed
35020	4237	353,256	Nine Elms	BROKEN	✱	BROKEN	flawed	flawed
35023	4174	386,033	Exmouth Junction	flawed	✱	flawed	flawed	flawed
35024	4183	397,182	Exmouth Junction	flawed	✱	flawed	flawed	flawed
35025	5251	220,831	Exmouth Junction	flawed	✱	flawed	clear	flawed
35026	5260	190,857	Stewarts Lane	–	flawed	NOT CONFIRMED		
35028	5278	166,151	Stewarts Lane	flawed	✱	flawed	flawed	flawed
35030	5296	151,982	Dover	flawed	✱	flawed	flawed	clear

✱ Supersonic test on the Web Seat not necessary, as the axle was withdrawn due to flaw under sprocket.

It couldn't happen now of course, there wouldn't be a service for three months as a tidal wave of health and safety recrimination swept over everyone involved, near or far. When, on 11 May it became clear that the Merchant Navys would have to come out of service 'that night' the other Regions were alerted and were rallying round, drumming up locos almost within hours. Less than two days later WR Britannias were at work and a day after that V2s of all things were also on Southern trains. And popular enough they were too – or at least they were not deeply unpopular. They seemed to have done the job well enough, but were not really considered the equal of the Bulleid. On 29 May 1953 60916, still bearing its New England shedplate, waited at Waterloo with the 5.30pm to Bournemouth, alongside 'certified' Exmouth Junction Merchant Navy 35023 HOLLAND-AFRIKA LINE. Photograph John Aylard.

Analysis

35020 had suffered a complete fracture of the cross section of that portion of the axle on which the sprocket was clamped. It was ascribed to 'progressive fatigue' which extended to six inches of the diameter. The remaining two and a half inches represented the sudden, disastrous failure. Microscopic examination and even looking with a hand lens betrayed bands of corrosion and fatigue cracking, though chemical and mechanical tests on the fractured axle found the steel to be of acceptable quality.

For detailed technical reasons the cause of failure was deemed to be 'fretting corrosion fatigue', a phenomenon which occurred at the contact between two highly loaded metals. The solution (the reader will appreciate that extreme para-phrasing is being employed here) was a re-design – temporarily at least – of the crank axle. Increasing the diameter of the axle portions between the crank webs and the journals by just three eighths of an inch reduced the stress at 80mph sufficiently to render the metal free of the damaging consequences. Modified cranks would be fitted to all the locomotives as soon as the sprockets were ready, 'to

alleviate the position'. After that new balanced cranks would be fitted but in the meantime, as there was no reliable guide to how cracking might have advanced (it was independent of mileage for instance) regular nine-monthly supersonic tests would be carried out at the sheds 'until such time' as the supply of material permitted balanced cranks to be fitted, or until further information warranted an alteration in the period between examinations. With that, the emergency was fading.

Fun All Round

During the temporary withdrawal of the MERCHANT NAVY Pacifics replacements were loaned by other Regions and for a short while observers on both the Western and Eastern Sections of the SR had an enjoyable time recording these visitors to their part of England. *The Railway Observer* for June 1953 gives an excellent account of these movements – on 13 May 1953 for instance, the WR sent Britannias 70017, 70023, 70024, 70028 and 70029 to Nine Elms while the LMR sent 70030 and 70034 to Stewarts Lane shed and, later, some Black Fives to Nine Elms. The ER came up with a number of V2s which

needed minor amendments to the cab steps and live steam injector pipe so they could work Waterloo-Exeter and via Sway to Bournemouth. These were 60893, 60896, 60908, 60916, 60917 and 60928. With some of the light Pacifics needing attention as well some more replacements were in order – three BR Standard class 5 4-6-0s and fifteen B1s from the ER. The work of these loaned engines involved Waterloo-Bournemouth duties including the Bournemouth Belle; Waterloo-Exeter; Waterloo-Basingstoke semi-fasts; goods work; Victoria to Ramsgate and Ashford with 70030 and 70034 noted on Boat Train duties. The temporary allocations were:-

Nine Elms: 45051, 45061, 45130, 45216, 45222, 45223, 45350, 60893, 60896, 60908, 60916, 60917, 60928, 73003, 73015, 73017.
Exmouth Jct: 70024, 70028, 70029.
Salisbury: 70017, 70023.
Stewarts Lane: 61015, 61041, 61050, 61109, 61133, 61138, 61148, 61188, 61192, 61219, 61273, 61274, 61329, 61338, 61354, 70034.
Dover: 70030.

The first Merchant Navy to be rebuilt was 35018 BRITISH INDIA LINE, coming into traffic in February 1956 – here it is taking shape in Eastleigh Works on 18 January 1956. Unlike other famous classes, such as the Royal Scots, these were genuine rebuilds, and not new locomotives under some accounting cloak. The *Report on Proposed Modifications* to the engines (see text) listed the features to be replaced – principally the valve gear/oil bath, smokebox and the casing, with the tender to be severely modified. The tender modification of course had seen the light of day as early as 1952 with three so treated and one more in 1953. The rest of the tenders were done from 1956, except where they were rebodied. The most obvious way in which the engines changed was of course in the removal of the casing and the remaking into a locomotive of conventional outline. The boiler and firebox, the excellent fundamentals of the design, were kept, along with the outside cylinders; the old fabricated smokebox with all its odd angles was done away with and replaced by a firmly conventional cylindrical one. The oval door kept the look of the original, and helped among many other things to make the new design distinctive, even though it was being made 'more conventional'. Photograph Les Elsey.

Flight of the Phoenix

Once Bulleid had gone from the Southern, in September 1949, there would be no more serious development of his Pacifics – in anything like their original form that is. The work of further testing (as described earlier) was done with the Rugby engine, 35022 HOLLAND-AMERICA LINE with single blastpipe and then without thermic syphons, and haulage trials were done on the Eastern Section, comparing a Merchant Navy with a light Pacific and a Britannia. No obviously lasting consequences seemed to derive from this and by 1954, though reliability had increased markedly since the dark early days, the unthinkable was being thought; would it be easier just to scrap the engines? The feeling had in fact been around since before the last of the Merchant Navys had been built (!) for a programme announced in 1946 predicted the end of all steam on the Southern by the middle 1950s. By 1954 it was clear that this would not be attained so rebuilding into a more conventional form figured increasingly in the Region's councils.

If the engines were to be scrapped, something would have to be built new to replace them, and this, logically, could only be another thirty Britannia Pacifics. With the boiler and firebox condition of the Merchant Navys specially checked and found to be rather good, the equation swung very much in favour of rebuilding. Much of the argument is contained in this report (which of course considers the light Pacifics too) made at Brighton in January 1955. Some of the details are alarming – there are no less than *thirty-eight* fires for 1953 alone for instance, though curiously they do not feature as a 'cause' under the 'Availability' table.

REPORT ON THE PROPOSED MODIFICATIONS TO THE 'MERCHANT NAVY' AND 'WEST COUNTRY' CLASSES OF LOCOMOTIVES

INTRODUCTION

The 'Merchant Navy' class of locomotive was introduced on the former Southern Railway in 1941 and 30 of this class were built in three batches between the years 1941 and 1949.

The 'West Country' class of locomotive, which includes the 'Battle of Britain' class, was brought out in 1945 and is similar, in all major respects to the 'Merchant Navy' class but is of less weight so as to be available for use on routes where the restrictions are more severe. Between 1945 and 1951 110 of this class of locomotive were built.

DESIGN

Although the locomotives follow the normal modern design tendencies for a Pacific type with three-cylinders and a wide firebox boiler, there are a number of features which are not usually employed in British locomotive practice, among which are:-

(i) Special valve gear, having a chain drive to a three-throw crank shaft, which drives valve gear for each of the three cylinders. Each gear is connected to the piston valve through a rocking arrangement having a 3:8 ratio, which in practice has proved to be unsatisfactory.

(ii) An oil bath enclosing the three sets of special valve gear and the inside motion. This is intended to give continuous lubrication to the working parts.

(iii) A smokebox, of irregular shape, as opposed to the more usual one of cylindrical form.

(iv) Special casing over the whole of the upper part of the locomotive described by the designer as 'air smoothing'.

PERFORMANCE

The locomotives, when hauling the principal express trains of the Region have demonstrated their ability to run to time with an ample margin of power, due to their excellent steaming properties, and free running characteristics. From availability and maintenance points of view, however, the locomotives are less satisfactory, whilst their consumption of coal, water and oil is high in relation to other modern locomotives.

The unsatisfactory features can be covered under four headings:- (i) running costs, (ii) reliability, (iii) availability, (iv) cost of repairs and maintenance.

(i) Running Costs
(a) Thermal Efficiency
Tests were conducted in 1951 and 1952 at

35017 BELGIAN MARINE nearing completion at the end of March 1957. L. Roberts would certainly have a tale to tell of these times – one of his ladders is still stashed on the cab floor. Photograph Collection John Fry.

Rugby and on the road between Carlisle and Skipton, with 'Merchant Navy' Class locomotive No.35022 and one of the BR Class 7 Pacifics. These tests have demonstrated that whereas there is no substantial difference in the boiler efficiency between the two classes, (actual average boiler efficiency of the 'Merchant Navy' in standard condition is only 1½% less than that of the Class 7) the cylinder thermal efficiency shows to disadvantage over a wide range of working as indicated by the following table 1:-

TABLE 1

Cylinder Thermal Efficiency - %

Steam rate lb/hour	14,000 (light working)			20,000 (Normal working)			28,000 (Very heavy working)		
Speed mph	20	40	60	20	40	60	20	40	60
Efficiency % Class 7 4-6-2	11.9	13.0	13.4	11.6	13.5	14.0	10.2	12.6	13.25
'Merchant Navy'	9.7	11.0	-	10.3	11.6	11.85	10.2	11.5	11.95
Reduction %	18.5	15.4	-	11.2	14.1	15.3	0	8.7	9.8

The lower thermal efficiency of the 'Merchant Navy' as compared with the BR class 7 4-6-2 (and with practically all other classes which have been tested) is due primarily to the inefficient utilisation of the steam in the cylinders. The fact that the superheat temperature of the 'Merchant Navy' is about 50°F lower than that of the Class 7 4-6-2 locomotive will have some effect, but in the main the lower thermal efficiency must be attributed to the faulty distribution of the steam by the valves.

Indicator cards taken during the Rugby tests have been examined and very erratic results have been shown. In some cases the indicator card may consist of a diagram of large area in one end of the cylinder whilst the other end may enclose practically no area at all. In other cases, diagrams of appreciably different shapes are obtained and different results are observed simultaneously in the three cylinders.

(b) Coal
In the road tests, results generally corroborative of those given above were obtained and for a direct comparison of operating economy, the comparable figures of coal consumed are as follows (Table 2):-

TABLE 2

Pounds of coal (Blidworth) per drawbar horsepower hour.

Speed mph	60			40		
Drawbar horsepower	800	1200	1600	800	1200	1600
C1.7 4-6-2	2.40	2.22	2.40	2.15	2.00	2.20
'Merchant Navy'	2.77	2.47	2.40	2.46	2.35	2.39
Increase %	15.4	11.3	0	14.4	17.5	8.6

The high consumptions of coal by these locomotives is also apparent from a comparison with other Regional classes. In the Interchange Trials of 1948 average figures were obtained running over all the routes (Table 3).
These figures show an increased consumption of 13% and 15% in the case of the 'Merchant Navy' and 'West Country' class locomotives respectively compared with similar class locomotives operating in other regions.

TABLE 4

Pounds of water per drawbar horsepower hour

Speed mph	60			40		
Drawbar horsepower	800	1200	1600	800	1200	1600
C1.7 4-6-2	20.2	17.4	17.2	18.3	16.2	16.2
'M. Navy'	23.2	19.6	17.9	21.0	18.9	17.8
Increase %	14.9	12.6	4.1	14.8	16.7	9.9

One other factor in high coal consumption of the 'West Country' class in ordinary service is the absence of damper doors on the ashpan, on all but the last twenty locomotives and three others which have been subsequently modified experimentally. Very skilful handling on the part of the fireman is necessary in order to avoid blowing off under these conditions and considering the youth and inexperience of many

TABLE 3

Pounds of coal per drawbar horsepower hour

Class of Locomotive	1
Express Passenger Types	
ER A4	3.06
LMR 'Duchess'	3.12
LMR 'Royal Scot'	3.38
Average	3.19
SR 'Merchant Navy'	3.60
Mixed Traffic Types	
ER B1	3.59
LM Class 5	3.54
Average	3.57
SR 'West Country'	4.11

1 = lb.coal/DB HP per hour

firemen who have to work on these locomotives today, it is unquestionable that unnecessary blowing off occurs, with consequent waste of coal and water.

(c) Water
The water consumption of a locomotive gives a measure of the cylinder efficiency and for any similar degree of superheat it is approximately true that the cylinder efficiency and the water per indicated horsepower hour are inversely proportional. The Rugby trials showed that the water consumption of the 'Merchant Navy' was high in relation to that of the BR Standard Class 7 Pacific. The following figures were obtained in the road tests between Carlisle and Skipton (Table 4 above).

These figures are in reasonable agreement with the results of the 1948 Interchange Trials in which the average water consumption of the 'Merchant Navy' class was approximately 18% higher than that of the average of the Eastern & North Eastern and LM regional classes.

(d) Oil
The oil consumption of the 'Merchant Navy' and 'West Country' locomotives is influenced principally by the provision of the oil bath for the valve gears and inside motion. It was intended that this arrangement would function as an oil circulating system which would require occasional topping up, instead of the system normally used on locomotives. In practice it has been found virtually impossible to make the oil bath oiltight. The net result of leakage from the oil baths is that, over a typical period of 18 months, the average consumption of high quality lubricating oil amounted to just over 2 gallons per 100 miles for the 140 locomotives, making a total annual use of 120,000 gallons. This is in addition to the 15 pints of engine and cylinder oil per 100 miles which is issued to enginemen and artisan staff. The comparable issue for a 'Lord Nelson' class locomotive is 9½ pints per 100 miles, which is the total required for the locomotive.

(ii) Reliability
As a result of investigations into the troubles and failures which have occurred with these locomotives, modifications have been introduced which have tended to improve their reliability. The principal features which have caused unreliability are:-
(a) valve gear
(b) oil bath
(c) air-smoothed casing
(d) smokebox and leading end of locomotive
(e) rocking grate on 'West Country' class.
These features have been unreliable throughout the whole life of the locomotives to date; some of the troubles have been lessened by modification, but the main sources of unreliability are inherent in the design.

(a) Valve Gear
In service, failure of the valve gear is a not infrequent occurrence, the principal causes being fracture of the rocker shafts,

fracture of driving chains, and damage to valves due to over-travel. These failures give rise to loss of availability and high cost of repairs at the depots and in outstation material.

(b) Oil Bath

The oil bath, apart from requiring constant attention in the form of topping up, makes maintenance at the depots more difficult as the big end and valve gear parts cannot be so readily examined. It has, moreover, proved very difficult to exclude water from the oil bath and when this gains access appreciable corrosion occurs on the motion parts.

(c) Air-smoothed Casing

Fires on orthodox locomotives are practically unknown, but are a frequent occurrence in the 'Merchant Navy' and 'West Country' classes, 38 cases being reported in 1953.

Most of these fires commence in the vicinity of the ashpan hopper doors, due to accumulation of oil-soaked inflammable matter and frequently spread to the boiler lagging plates and clothing. The latter tend to become soaked in oil which presumably condenses from vapour escaping from the oil-bath. The shape of the air-smoothed casing tends to trap heat from the engine and set up temperature conditions approximately of the same order as the flash-point of the oil, so that once a fire starts, combustion can proceed readily under the casing, which forms a furnace. In cases where fires have gained a firm hold not only have the casing and paintwork been badly scorched, but the 'Yorkshire' joints in the lubricator pipes have been melted out, necessitating the withdrawal of the locomotive from traffic for repairs. Modifications have been made in the hope of reducing the tendency for the fires to spread to the boiler lagging. Clothing plates have been fitted to the underside of the boiler barrel, but nevertheless it has not been possible to prevent the occurrence of fires.

The air-smoothed casing is troublesome to maintain and great care is required to prevent parts from becoming detached. It has proved particularly difficult to fix the doors which are needed to allow of access to sanding fillers, whistle valve etc. The 'air smoothed' casing unquestionably makes more work at motive power depots as parts requiring attention are generally hidden and removal of part of the casing is often necessary, or the work can only be carried out under difficulties.

(d) Smokebox and leading end of locomotive

The frames of the locomotives have behaved very well, the only trouble experienced being at the leading end of the 'West Country' class at the front of the inside cylinder where there is a common line of bolts with the back flange of the outside cylinders. To combat this trouble a stronger stretcher and additional horizontal and vertical plate stretchers between the outside cylinders, have been fitted. In spite of this alteration, however, there is still a measurable amount of frame torsion which gives rise to trouble with the main steam pipes in the smokebox. Leakage at this point and at the stuffing box, where the steam pipe enters the smokebox, has

TABLE 5

Region	Class	Pence per engine mile			
		Engines (Between General Repairs)	Boilers	Tenders (Between Repairs)	Total Engines, boilers and tenders
SR	Merchant Navy	10.692	2.145	0.870	13.707
	West Country	10.571	2.579	0.861	14.011
	Lord Nelson	7.107	0.516	1.021	8.644
ER, NER	A1	5.623	0.587	0.797	7.007
	A4	7.967	0.936	0.673	9.576
	A2/3	7.101	0.990	0.797	8.888
LM	Coronation	7.967	0.936	0.673	9.576

a very detrimental effect upon the steaming.

(e) Rocking grate on 'West Country' class locomotive

The design of the grate on the 'West Country' class gives rise to a great deal of trouble. The grate is of the rocking type, with a 'drop' section, the latter having rocking bars mounted in it. In consequence of its unreliability, the grate is little used in the manner intended, since experience of the grates collapsing, following use either for rocking or firedropping, has produced a feeling of lack of confidence in it.

(iii) Availability

The number of weekdays out of service for running repairs and examinations in 1952 for the 'Merchant Navy', 'West Country' and 'Lord Nelson' Classes are given below. These figures are extracted from the return rendered by the Locomotive Accountant, headed 'Costing of Locomotive Repairs, Annual Mileage & Weekdays out of Service.

'Merchant Navy' class 61.69 weekdays out of service.
'West Country' class 53.95 weekdays out of service.
'Lord Nelson' class 49.38 weekdays out of service.

Specially kept records show that the number of weekdays lost to service on account of engine defects at sheds in 1953 for the 140 locomotives, from all causes was 5,501 or 39.3 days per engine. Of these the following totals were attributable to individual causes:-

Valve gear 1,021 days
Valves and Pistons 251 days
Steam and Exhaust pipes 423 days
Grates and Ashpans 215 days
Steam reversing gear 50 days

(iv) Cost of Repair and Maintenance

The cost of maintenance of these locomotives is materially influenced by the considerations set out under (ii) and (iii) - Reliability and Availability.

The following statement is taken from Appendix F of Individual costing of locomotive repairs returns for the three years 1950-1952, headed 'Classified repairs to selected locomotives at Workshops and Motive Power depots'. The cost of repair in pence per engine mile is shown for three classes of Southern Region locomotives and also for comparable 'Pacific' classes from other Regions. Table 5 (top) refers.

In the Works, considerably more man-

hours are required for intermediate and general repairs to the Merchant Navy and West Country class locomotives than for other locomotives of approximately comparable size and power. The cost of general and intermediate repairs to engines and tenders (excluding work on the boilers) to 'Merchant Navy' and 'West Country' class locomotives is 20% more than comparable repairs of 'Lord Nelson' class locomotives, as shown by the following figures taken from the individual costing of locomotive returns:-

Total Cost of 41 General and Heavy Intermediate repairs to 'Merchant Navy' and 'West Country' class locomotives (Period 5/50 to 12/53) = £132,812
Average per repair = £3,239

Total Cost of 12 General or Heavy Intermediate repairs to 'Lord Nelson' class locomotives (Period 5/50 to 12/53) = £32,370
Average per repair = £2,697

Increased cost of repair of 'Merchant Navy' and 'West Country' class locomotives compared with the 'Lord Nelson' class locomotives = £542 = 20% (These costs have been equated to 1954 price levels)

This difference is accounted for largely by (1) the work involved in removing the air-smoothed casing before the essential parts of the locomotive can be stripped and its replacement after repairs have been carried out and (2) the complexity of the valve gear and its associated parts including the oil bath and the extent of wear and tear on those and the need for much renovation and renewal.

PROPOSAL TO MODIFY THE LOCOMOTIVES

Three 'Merchant Navy' and three 'West Country' class locomotives have recently been modified in a number of respects, in an endeavour to eliminate as many as possible of the troublesome features of the locomotives short of a major modification. Some improvement has been shown in the case of the parts actually modified. In addition, various modifications have been made to individual components, when it has been necessary to replace them.

The proposal now put forward will virtually eliminate the principal troublesome features and will bring the running costs into line with those of the

BRITISH INDIA LINE weeks from unveiling, late in January 1956. Three sets of Walschaerts valve gear to replace Bulleid's chain driven motion necessitated a new inside admission middle cylinder. For economy the two outside cylinders were retained with their outside admission. This is why the rebuilds could often be found with steam escaping from around these cylinders. A rocking grate was provided, with six moveable sections each side of the centre line. Each section was operated manually. Plain section coupling rods instead of the I section ones were fitted to combat buckling when slipping. The mechanical lubricators for cylinder valve chests were moved from their awkward and ash-prone site below the smokebox frontplate up on to the running plate above

the front drivers, two on the left and one on the right. A fourth was added on the right-hand side to supply oil to the cylinders and leading axleboxes. This superseded the multifeed boxes (or 'trays') in the cab. Other modifications included reverse sanding on the middle driver (see elsewhere) and different intermediate drawgear between engine and tender. The drawbar was now pin jointed to the tender by means of a plunger sliding freely in guides and controlled by the intermediate drawbar rubber spring, which cushioned the pull. When Bulleid was shown photographs of the rebuilt 35018 and asked his opinion he replied, characteristically, that if he thought them better that way, he'd have done them like that himself! Photograph Collection John Fry.

other principal express passenger locomotives without impairing their performance in any way and increase the availability, while reducing the maintenance in Shops and Motive Power Depots.

The proposal involves the retention of the boiler, frames, outside cylinders, wheels, axleboxes etc and the replacement or removal of the following existing components:-

(i)   Special valve gear and rocker shafts.
(ii)   Inside cylinder.
(iii)   Smokebox, superheater header, steampipes etc.
(iv)   Reversing gear.
(v)   Piston heads and rods.
(vi)   Oil bath.
(vii)   Air-smoothed casing.
(viii) Mechanical lubricators.
(ix)   Regulator.
(x)   Ashpan and grate.
(xi)   Cylinder Cocks
(xii)   Sandboxes.
(xiii) Tender. (a) raves and provision of tunnel for fire irons.

(b) tank sieves.
(c) water level gauge.
(d) intermediate drawbar.

Account has been taken in the financial statement of those components on the above list, which would require replacement or repair during the shop overhauls at which the modified components will be fitted.

The main points in the design of the components which will replace the twelve components (i)-(xii) listed above are given below:-

<u>*(i) Valve Gear*</u>
The main purpose of the modifications is to provide the locomotive with three independent sets of Walschaerts valve gear of a type which has been well proved and which is known to give a very good steam distribution. The cylinder efficiency will then be brought into line with other modern steam locomotives. The two outside sets of valve gear will be similar to those of the standard Class 4

2-6-4 tank locomotives and the inside valve gear will follow the design of the Southern Region 'Schools' class. Two new driving crank pins will be provided to take the return cranks. An eccentric will be placed on the crank axle in place of the existing chain-driving sprocket. Provision was made for this latter modification when the crank axle was re-designed, following upon the failures of the crank axles which were the subject of my report of January 1954.

<u>*(ii) Inside Cylinder*</u>
Forward of the inside cylinder (which will have a piston valve with inside admission), and bolted to it, will be a saddle. These two components will butt up to the existing stretchers and give a very strong construction, which will eliminate the frame fractures which have been experienced at the leading end of the 'West Country' class.

<u>*(iii) Smokebox, Superheater header and*</u>

Steam pipes
A circular smokebox, fitted to the saddle, will ensure a robust construction, which will remove the troubles experienced with the present design of steam pipes and stuffing boxes. The latter will be similar to those on the standard locomotives. A new header will be required to suit the circular smokebox, but the existing smokebox door will be retained.

(iv) Reversing gear
The reversing gear will consist of one shaft for both inside and outside valve gears, operated by means of a screw. This type of gear will enable fine adjustments of the cut-off to be made and will result in the locomotives being worked at an early cut off with a degree of certainty not possible with the steam reversing gear.

(v) Piston heads and rods
It is proposed to replace the existing type of piston heads, having a coned attachment to the piston rod, by parallel fastened heads of the type used on the BR Standard locomotives. A good deal of trouble has been experienced in the past due to the piston heads becoming loose and the BR type of attachment will eliminate this trouble. The new piston rods will be fitted to separate crossheads and this will enable the piston heads and rods to be removed out of the front of the cylinders as one unit in the normal manner.

(vi) Oil bath
The elimination of the oil bath will make the examination of the inside big end and motion much easier and the trouble which has been experienced of rusting of pins and gear will cease. This will be beneficial from the point of view of cleanliness of the underside of the locomotive and also in regard to slipping, as with the present arrangement a lot of oil finds its way on to the driving wheel treads. The Civil Engineer will also be relieved of certain maintenance since at the present time the loss of oil to the ballast is a source of embarrassment to him.

(vii) Boiler Clothing
The normal type of clothing will be fitted to the boiler which, together with the removal of the oil bath, will eliminate the trouble which has been experienced of fires occurring in oil saturated boiler clothing mattresses. Many details, particularly pipework, will be far more accessible than heretofore. Opportunity will be taken to provide footplating along the side of the engine.

(viii) Mechanical Lubricators
Two new mechanical lubricators will be used for the lubrication of the cylinders and axleboxes, and will be mounted at suitable positions on the motion brackets and driven in the usual manner. If the three existing mechanical lubricators which lubricate the cylinders and which are mounted in front of the smokebox were used, it would be necessary to increase this number to four in order to include the axleboxes; experience shows that with a number of lubricators to fill, one is very liable to be missed. The existing mechanical lubricators will be fitted to other classes of locomotives.

The use of a mechanical lubricator for the axleboxes will considerably reduce

the length of copper piping, which must, of necessity, be used with the existing method of lubrication by a large trimming fed oilbox mounted on the cab.

(ix) Regulator
The existing regulator will be replaced by one of the horizontal grid type, arranged in such a way as to give a well graduated opening, in order to reduce the tendency of the locomotives to slip.

(x) Ashpan and Grate
Both classes of locomotive will be fitted with new ashpans with hopper bottom doors and front and rear damper doors. The fitting of dampers will improve, as far as the 'West Country' class is concerned, the control which can be exercised on the fire in order to prevent blowing off. The ashpans will be self-discharging to a greater extent than those now fitted and will therefore assist in the disposal of the locomotives.

(xi) Cylinder Cocks
The existing coned plug type of cylinder cock has proved expensive to maintain in a proper state of repair and the poppet type will be fitted in its place.

(xii) Sandboxes
New sandboxes will be provided and fitted, where possible, between the frames.

(xiii)Tender
(a) Raves and provision of tunnels for fire irons
Reference has been made in paragraph 1 of the section above headed 'PROPOSAL TO MODIFY THE LOCOMOTIVES' to the modifications which have been made to three locomotives of each class. Included in these modifications were the removal of the raves and the provision of tunnels for fire irons and covers over vacuum brake reservoirs.

The Motive Power Superintendent is satisfied that there is an improvement in the coaling and taking of water of these modified tenders. He also states that previous to the provision of the tunnel for the fire irons, it was necessary periodically for shed staff to clear the coal from the side troughs in order that the fire irons could be safely retained on the pegs provided.

These modifications will be carried out on the remainder of the tenders of these two classes of locomotives.

(b) Tank Sieves
The strainers as originally fitted on these tenders did not provide a positive means of preventing foreign matter, principally particles of coal, from passing from the tender tank along the feed pipes. This resulted in the failure of the injectors. An improvement has been made to the existing strainers, but they are not entirely satisfactory and must be cleaned at regular intervals. The cleaning involves the emptying of the tank, since it is necessary for staff

to enter the tank for this purpose.

Sieves located in boxes mounted external to the tank will now be fitted, following the design on BR locomotives. The boxes can be shut off from the tank, enabling the strainers to be cleaned without the necessity of emptying the water from the tank.

(c) Water level gauge
The existing water level indicator is of primitive design, consisting of a vertical tube with small holes located at intervals throughout its height. The indicator has been generally un-satisfactory either due to the water valve being difficult to operate or to the small holes becoming blocked. The BR type of water level indicator will be fitted.

(d) Intermediate drawbar
Over 90% of the drawbars on the locomotives of these classes entering the works are found to be flawed when magnetically tested and are replaced. The trouble has been traced to two features of the drawgear which tend to induce very high stresses in the components:-
(i) The use of a curved rubbing block on the tender, which rubs against a flat block on the engine drag beam. On a reverse curve this arrangement produces a large stroke of the drawbar spring with the consequent high loading of the drawbar. Tests have shown that where both rubbing blocks are suitably curved this effect can be eliminated.
(ii) The use of a spherical bearing surface at the point where the load in the drawbar is transmitted to the tender underframe, in front of the drawbar spring. Experience of spherical surfaces generally has shown them to be unsatisfactory as there is a high resistance to movement with consequent imposition of bending stresses in the drawbar.

In order to prevent the possibility of engine and tender parting in service, all the locomotives have now been fitted with safety links.

The drawgear will be modified to include curved rubbing blocks and the replacement of the spherical bearing surface by a pin joint, similar in principle to the design in use on the Eastern and Northern Eastern regional locomotives.

PROGRAMME FOR THE CONVERSION OF THE LOCOMOTIVES

It is proposed that the 30 'Merchant Navy' class locomotives should first be modified,

TABLE 6 COAL, WATER AND OIL	30 'MN' Locos	110 'WC' and B of B'
Coal @ 3lb per mile		
2,010 tons @ 78/6d per ton	£7,889	-
6,350 tons @ 78/6d per ton	-	£24,924
Water @ 3 gallons per mile		
4,500,000 galls @ 2/3d per 1,000 (treated)	£506	-
14,200,000 galls @ 2/3d per 1,000 (treated)	-	£1,598
Oil @ 2 gallons per 100 miles		
30,000 galls @ 2/3d	£3,375	-
94,000 galls @ 2/3d	-	£10,642
	£11,770	£37,164
	======	======

followed by the 110 'West Country' class. Drawings can be prepared in such time as will enable six 'Merchant Navy' class locomotives to be modified during 1955, the remainder of the locomotives being covered at the rate of 24 per year during 1956 and the following years, until the completion of the work in 1961.

FINANCIAL ASPECT OF PROPOSED MODIFICATIONS

The gross outlay involved in the proposed modifications is £5,615 per locomotive.

Operating Savings
The operative savings that can be expected from the proposed modifications have been discussed with the Motive Power Superintendent and he has agreed that the following annual savings will accrue. (Table 6 below) :-

The annual mileage per locomotive on which these savings are based are 50,000 and 43,000 for the 'Merchant Navy' and 'West Country' classes respectively. These figures are taken from the return 'Locomotives - Annual Mileage and Analysis of Weekdays for Year 1952' which is compiled by the Locomotive Accountant.

Staff
When all 140 locomotives have been modified there will be a saving of ten Grade 1 fitters and seventeen fitters' assistants Group 4, with a financial saving of £13,650 per annum in the Motive Power Superintendent's department.

Availability
The increased availability of the modified locomotives will no doubt make possible a small reduction in the number of locomotives required on the region, provided that the workings remain the same as at present. The class and number of the locomotives will be decided when the modification to the 'Merchant Navy'

and 'West Country' class locomotives has been completed.

Savings at Main Workshops
The repair savings at General and Intermediate repairs at the Main Workshops are estimated at £445 per repair.

Summary
The Regional Accountant has been consulted and a copy of his memorandum setting out the financial aspect of the scheme is attached. This shows that the total estimated net saving up to the assumed date of scrapping of the locomotives, before taking account of the interest factor is £2,051,402. Bringing interest into the calculations produces an equivalent capital sum as at 1955 of approximately £850,000.

Authority is required for an amount of £760,400 made up as under:-

	£
Gross outlay	786,100
Less: estimated recoveries	25,700
	£760,400

Chief Mechanical & Electrical Engineer's Office
BRIGHTON
January 1955

***

Thus was the case made. In due course, in February 1956, a very different Merchant Navy indeed emerged from Eastleigh Works, 35018 BRITISH INDIA LINE. Its first days turned out to be slightly less auspicious than the authorities would have liked... It was in the Works Yard for official inspection on 9 February 1956 and the following day ran a trial trip to Botley and back.

On 12 February it set off for Nine Elms and inspection at Waterloo by Sir Brian Robertson the next day. BRITISH INDIA LINE returned to Eastleigh on 14 February and on the 17th was rostered for its first passenger work proper, Eastleigh shed duty 253, taking over the 9.54am train from Waterloo and the 1.29pm Fareham-Bournemouth West at Southampton Central. A glorious debut it was not to be, however, and it was afterwards noted dead at St Denys, being hauled tender first by M7 0-4-4T 30376. BR Class 5 73052, itself bound for shopping at Eastleigh, took over 35018's train. The failure, recorded *The Railway Observer* (here a rueful smile might have appeared in some quarters) was 'believed to be due to a lubrication fault'...

BRITISH INDIA LINE was soon back in action, running a trial to Botley and back on 20 February and then resuming work on duty 253 until the 27th, when it failed, immobilised at Farnborough with radius rod trouble. It was dragged to Eastleigh Works again and once the clearances were opened out 35018 worked away happily, with only a short one day works check-up – these visits were not noted on the Record Card. It was telling, and indicative of the contradictions in the class, that at the same time, while 35018 was feeling its way (including a few turns on the Bournemouth Belle) some of its fellows in original condition were putting up perfectly exhilarating performances. On 14 April for instance, as *The Railway Observer* recorded, 35021 rolled into Salisbury with the down Atlantic Coast Express six

Pacifics were in and out of Eastleigh throughout the rest of the 1950s after BRITISH INDIA LINE at the beginning of 1956. This is 35020 BIBBY LINE which had once tried to lay waste to Crewkerne station and very sparkling it looks too, taking shape as 'a rebuild' in April 1956. All the pieces are coming together, such as firehole doors chalked up 35020, with much of the pipework and firebox fittings waiting attachment. The work depended to a great extent on the humble wooden ladder, and all the ones around are carefully painted with its owner's name – *L. ROBERTS ERECTING SHOP* – to stop them being 'borrowed'. Mr Roberts was one of the three Erecting Shop chargehands involved with the rebuilding. Photograph Collection John Fry.

minutes early with a train seventy tons over the 'norm' – *'to the astonishment of the station staff and relief engine crew'*. By 8 May 1956 the second rebuild, 35020 BIBBY LINE was limbering up on its running in turns. What follows (opposite) is the 'Financial Memorandum' mentioned in the *Summary* of the Report above, setting out in more detail some of the financial figures (look at some of the projected dates for the demise of the Pacifics...)

FINANCIAL MEMORANDUM
'Merchant Navy' and 'West Country' and 'Battle of Britain' class locomotives:

TABLE 1

	30'MN' Locomotives and Tenders	110 'WC/BB' Locomotives and Tenders	Total 140 Locomotives
Anticipated net expenditure on alterations	£146,600	£ 541,250	£687,850
Anticipated savings in maintenance and operating costs	£455,383	£2,283,869	£2,739,252
Anticipated net savings	£308,783	£1,742,619	£2,051,402

General - all expenditure is at 1954 price level

Anticipated net expenditure on alteration is made up of:-

	30 'MN' Locomotives and Tenders	110 'WC/BB' Locomotives and Tenders	Total 140 Locomotives
Gross outlay @ £5,615 each	£168,450	£617,650	£786,100
Less recoveries during alterations	£ 5,500	£20,200	£25,700
Amount for which authority is sought	£162,950	£597,450	£760,400
Less cost of repairs avoided	£16,350	£56,200	£72,550
Net additional outlay (estimated on prime cost bases supplied by CM & EE Department)	146,600	541,250	687,850

proposed modifications to Valve Gear and other parts on engines and modifications to tenders.

The scheme provides for an estimated net expenditure of £687,850 in the years 1955 to 1961 on the alterations to the engines and tenders and will result in estimated savings in maintenance and operating costs, up to the assumed date of scrapping, of £2,739,252 in years 1955 to 1987, i.e. a net estimated ultimate saving of £2,051,402, ignoring the factor of interest, which is considered in the conclusion.

The figures for the separate schemes are set out above in Table 1:

SAVINGS
In order to assess these, it has been necessary to make assumptions as to when the expenditure will be incurred and when the resulting savings will fructify.

It has been assumed that the output of converted locomotives will be equally spread from October 1955 to July 1961 inclusive; that certain preparatory expenditure will be incurred in 1955; and that the last 12 months (1960/61) expenditure will be correspondingly reduced.

On this basis and a periodicity between repairs (general and intermediate) of eighteen months, it has been assumed that partial repair economies will result in the second half of 1955, and continue until the locomotives are

withdrawn from service, but will not reach their maximum until 1962.

Similarly, on the above basis of output it has been assumed that operating savings will begin to accrue in 1955 (for three months) in respect of 50% of the output of that period and again reach their maximum and continuing figure in 1962.

The repair savings have been assessed firstly on the basis of prime costs factors supplied by the Works Manager at Eastleigh, at £445 per repair (for variable costs only). It has been assumed that these savings will commence in 1957 and attain maximum in 1962.

Secondly, the Motive Power Superintendent estimates that, as a result of rebuilding of these Locomotives, he will save

TABLE 2

	30 'MN'	110 'WC/BB'
Coal @ 3lb per mile		-
2,010 tons @ 78/6d per ton	£7,889	£24,924
6,350 tons @ 78/6d per ton	-	
Water @ 3 gallons per mile		
4,500,000 gallons 2/3d per 1,000 (treated)	£506	-
14,200,000 gallons @ 2/3d per 1,000 (treated)	-	£1,598
Oil @ 2 gallons per 100 miles		-
30,000 galls @ 2/3d	£3,375	£10,642
94,600 galls @ 2/3d	-	
	£11,770	£37,164

ten fitters, grade 1 and seventeen fitters assistants, grade 4, with a total saving of £13,650 per annum, which includes overtime and Sunday working. This has been apportioned £2,925 against 'Merchant Navy' and £10,725 against the 'West Country' and 'Battle of Britain'; the saving being deemed to commence in 1955 and reach a maximum in 1962.

The maximum annual operating savings are made up as shown in Table 2 (bottom).

CONCLUSION
From the appendices it will be seen that, on the basis of the figures as they stand, the whole cost will be recovered by the year 1962 for 'Merchant Navy' locomotives and by the year 1966 for 'West Country' and 'Battle of Britain' locomotives.

As shown in the first two paragraphs the total estimated net saving up to the assumed date of scrapping of the locomotives, before taking account of the interest factor, is £2,051,402. Bringing interest into the calculations produces an equivalent capital sum as at 1955 of approximately £850,000.

It will be understood that if the cost of the work increases by price level or other causes and the savings do not increase pro rata, the period of complete recovery of outlay will be delayed and the total savings will be reduced. Appendix 'A' see overleaf

For J W J Webb
(Intld) RWK
Regional Accountant's Office
Deepdene House
DORKING
10 January 1955

A Cautionary Note
While these reports and estimates throw much valuable light on the thinking of the time, they are, in reality, 'archaeological' fragments only, illuminating in the way fossils are illuminating – they allow a fairly convincing picture to be drawn but they fall far short of revealing everything, and new evidence might always be around the next corner. There were other (protracted) suggestions as to what to do with the Bulleids, for instance, envisaging replace-ment of the valve gear only (with Walschaerts) and leaving the engines otherwise unchanged. Even in the 'might have been' stakes the Merchant Navys out-complicate other classes!

Regarding the reports above, it must be said that while it is all very well producing estimates to show savings, the only truly worthwhile figures are those based on what *really*

APPENDIX 'A'
30 'MERCHANT NAVY' LOCOMOTIVES

Expenditure on Alterations			Savings in Maintenance & Operating Costs up to assumed date of scrapping				
Year	Current Expenditure	Aggregate Expenditure	Year	Maintenance	Operating	Total	Aggregate Saving
	£	£		£	£	£	£
1955	72,992	72,992	1955	284	294	578	578
	73,608	146,600	1956	1,706	7,062	8,768	9,346
			1957	9,557	11,770	21,327	30,673
			1958	11,825	11,770	23,595	54,268
			1959	11,825	11,770	23,595	77,863
			1960	11,825	11,770	23,595	101,458
			1961	11,825	11,770	23,595	125,053
			1962	11,825	11,770	23,595	148,648*
			1963	11,825	11,770	23,595	172,243
			1964	11,825	11,770	23,595	195,838
			1965	11,825	11,770	23,595	219,433
			1966	11,825	11,770	23,595	243,028
			1967	11,825	11,770	23,595	266,623
			1968	11,825	11,770	23,595	290,218
			1969	11,825	11,770	23,595	313,813
			1970	11,825	11,770	23,595	337,408
			1971	11,825	11,770	23,595	361,003
			1972	11,825	11,770	23,595	384,598
			1973	11,825	11,770	23,595	408,193
			1974	11,825	11,770	23,595	431,788
			1975	11,825	11,770	23,595	455,383
		146,600		224,397	230,986	455,383	

Point where saving overtakes expenditure ignoring interest.

ensued. The rebuilt engines certainly had some very good strong features but it would be wrong to suggest they were a bed of roses. There was a design fault with the outside piston valve spindles for instance on the first fifty (Merchant Navys and light Pacifics) that called for some re-design work. Even so, as maintenance standards declined the high pressure glands at both ends of the outside steamchests caused problems. Steam leakage then took place on a massive scale. Roughness could also develop more rapidly, some of the 'converteds' seeming to knock themselves to pieces after a few years. In the rough and tumble of ordinary service coal saving turned out to be minimal – when driven with gusto the rebuilds could throw fires out of the chimney with the best of 'em. Crews, certainly, did not find the rebuilt engines an obvious 'leap forward', far from it. And don't forget the introductory note of the 1955 Report; the original engines *'have demonstrated their ability to run to time with an ample margin of power, due to their excellent steaming properties, and free running character-istics'*. Now *that* was what crews were interested in.

It is perhaps useful to quote Bulleid himself, when contemplating the projected savings from the rebuilding episode. He remarked that, while every defect that could be levied against his engines was taken into account when costing their limitations, for the rebuilds the savings were based on hoped-for achievements only. It is also useful to recall W. Marsh, the Southern's Assistant for Administration and Accounts, who studied the Reports on savings expected by the Regional Accountant in accordance with the BR (ex-LMS) standard method. Marsh did not wholly agree with the LMR methods and submitted his own workings which were less favourable to the project. This was (inevitably?) overruled.

MN	ORIGINAL FORM			REBUILT FORM			Best Utilisation when
	Years/ Months	Mileage	Yearly average	Years/ Months	Mileage	Yearly Average	
35001	18 6	807318	43639	5 3	288566	54965	Rebuilt
35002	16 11	776797	45919	5 9	325117	56542	Rebuilt
35003	17 11	859784	47988	7 11	272009	34359	Original
35004	16 9	750880	44829	7 3	378537	52212	Rebuilt
35005	17 5	632322	36306	7 5	344484	46447	Rebuilt
35006	17 10	862757	48379	4 10	271562	56185	Rebuilt
35007	15 11	799299	50218	9 2	519466	56690	Rebuilt
35008	14 11	730712	48986	10 2	555706	54660	Rebuilt
35009	14 9	684482	46406	7 2	442970	61810	Rebuilt
35010	14 6	663174	45736	9 8	578775	59873	Rebuilt
35011	14 7	670782	45996	6 7	398346	60508	Rebuilt
35012	12 1	564821	46744	10 2	570015	56067	Rebuilt
35013	11 3	517915	46037	11 2	596743	53440	Rebuilt
35014	11 5	516811	45268	10 8	545583	51148	Rebuilt
35015	13 3	549700	41487	5 8	264250	46630	Rebuilt
35016	12 1	467091	38656	8 4	433456	52026	Rebuilt
35017	11 11	594522	49890	9 4	423232	45346	Original
35018	10 9	504900	46967	8 6	451644	53135	Rebuilt
35019	13 11	617368	44362	6 4	329976	52101	Rebuilt
35020	10 10	507958	46888	8 10	473521	53606	Rebuilt
35021	10 9	575993	53581	6 2	283668	46000	Original
35022	7 8	329083	42924	9 11	574459	57929	Rebuilt
35023	8 3	433833	52586	10 5	507493	48719	Original
35024	10 5	552053	52162	5 9	287362	49976	Original
35025	8 1	419374	51881	7 9	420041	54199	Rebuilt
35026	8 1	311063	38482	10 2	547721	53874	Rebuilt
35027	8 5	363351	43170	9 4	508939	54529	Rebuilt
35028	10 10	401005	37016	7 9	393386	50759	Rebuilt
35029	10 7	428621	42862	7 0	319722	45675	Rebuilt
35030	9 0	351234	39026	9 3	499642	54015	Rebuilt
Averages	12 8	574833	45480	8 1	426883	52447	Rebuilt

Improvement in Utilisation by Rebuilding, overall = 15%

Table prepared by E.S. Youldon and first published in the journal of the Bulleid Society, *The Leader*.

Rebuilding Dates
35001 8/59
35002 5/58
35003 8/59
35004 7/58
35005 5/59
35006 10/59
35007 5/58
35008 5/57
35009 3/57
35010 1/57
35011 7/59
35012 2/57
35013 5/56
35014 7/56
35015 6/58
35016 4/57
35017 3/57
35018 2/56
35019 5/59
35020 4/56
35021 6/59
35022 6/56
35023 2/57

35024 4/59
35025 12/56
35026 1/57
35027 5/57
35028 10/59
35029 9/59
35030 4/58

ATC/AWS

Along with other BR express classes, the Merchant Navys began to get the Automatic Train Control, later designated Automatic Warning System; this was started on the Southern in 1959 and the first Merchant Navy so fitted, appropriately, was 35001 CHANNEL PACKET, in August 1960. The others followed at intervals thereafter. The battery box was sited prominently at the front above the buffer beam. Other equipment was inside, out of sight between the frames.

Liveries

Given their pedigree in all other respects, it might be assumed that the Merchant Navy liveries would be hideously complicated. This, fortunately, proves not to be the case; well, not much...

Coming out new in wartime did not help but the first engines, 21C1-21C6, carried the malachite green livery with three horizontal yellow bands. Economic constraints meant they were soon in black, along with the final ones of the first series, 21C8-21C10. 21C2 had emerged new in unlined malachite for trials but returned to Eastleigh to get the full lined livery. 21C7 too came out briefly with unlined malachite green, for works trials only before returning to works to emerge, in its turn, in black, which had just been introduced as the standard livery for all SR engines. The second batch too came out in wartime and 21C11-21C20 were accordingly garbed in black.

To black livery:-
21C1 1/44; 21C2 5/44; 21C3 5/43; 21C4 7/43; 21C5 3/42; 21C6 5/42; 21C7 6/42.
Black from new:-
21C8 6/42; 21C9 6/42; 21C10 7/42. 21C11 12/44; 21C12 1/45; 21C13 2/45; 21C14 2/45; 21C15 3/45; 21C16 3/45; 21C17 4/45; 21C18 5/45; 21C19 6/45; 21C20 6/45.

After the War the restoration of malachite green livery was the first step back to normality for the class, though Nationalisation made for further alterations.

From black to malachite green livery at the War's end and after:-
21C1 12/45; 21C2 7/46; 21C3 11/45; 21C4 4/46; 21C5 1/46; 21C6 9/46; 21C7 7/47; 21C8 8/47; 21C9 11/46; 21C10 6/47; 21C11 1/47; 21C12 4/45 (repainted grey from 2/45); 21C13

11/46; 21C14 11/45; 21C15 9/45; 21C16 1/47; 21C17 10/45; 21C18 8/45; 21C19 9/45; 21C20 8/45.
The third series, 35021-35030, had the following liveries from new:
unlined malachite green (the malachite, incidentally, wore rather badly): 35021 9/48 (lining added

11/48); 35022 10/48; 35024 11/48; 35026 12/48; 35027 12/48.
lined malachite green: 35023 11/48; 35025 11/48; 35028 12/48; 35029 2/49; 35030 4/49.

The reason for 35021, 35022, 35024, 35026 and 35027 coming out in

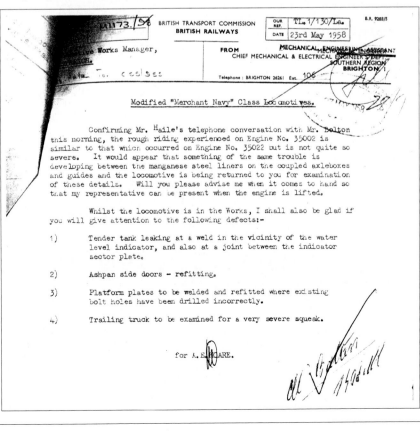

unfinished (i.e. unlined) malachite was because they were the ones attached to light Pacific tenders. When, one by one, they got their proper 6,000 gallon tenders, they received full liveries as follows:

35021 to full malachite 11/48 (6,000 gallon tender attached)
35022 to full malachite 1/49 (6,000 gallon tender attached)
35024 to experimental blue 2/49 (6,000 gallon tender attached)
35026 to standard blue 7/49 (6,000 gallon tender attached)
35027 to full malachite 4/49 (6,000 gallon tender attached)

35024 had quite a history of its own so far as early liveries were concerned:
13/11/48   New in unlined green (as above)
12/2/49   Experimental blue with three crimson lines. The blue encompassed wheels and skirting. Hand painted lion on wheel emblem.
29/3/49   Three crimson lines replaced by two black lines edged in white. Front skirting black together with cylinders.
30/4/49   Black skirting now continued throughout length of engine and tender. Wheels black. This now became the standard blue livery for the class.

With the formation of British Railways there were various experiments as to which liveries would suit which type of locomotive. For a while the majority of the Merchant Navys were painted dark blue; this appeared in February 1949 with horizontal red bands on 35024 EAST ASIATIC COMPANY*. These bands were promptly replaced by two lines in black with a fine white

---

35024 was the only one with red bands – it was, at the time, an experimental livery.

---

lining and later black wheels and a '...narrow black splash skirt'. Next for this treatment was 35026 LAMPORT & HOLT LINE in July 1949 when blue became the 'standard'. 35011, 35014 and 35023 were never painted blue, however, while 35001, 35017, 35024, 35026, and 35029 got blue twice each.

Dates repainted in the standard BR blue:-
35001 10/49;   35002 1/50; 35003 6/50; 35004 10/50;   35005 2/50; 35006 3/51; 35007 3/50; 35008 7/49; 35009 8/49; 35010   11/49;   35012 2/51; 35013 8/50; 35015 2/51; 35016 5/50; 35017 7/49; 35018 9/49; 35019 1/50; 35020 5/50; 35021 11/50; 35022   6/50; 35024 4/49; 35025 9/49; 35026 7/49; 35027 4/50; 35028 1/51; 35029 2/51; 35030 5/50.

Blue unfortunately proved a poor second to the malachite green both in appearance and expense – blue cannot wear like other colours it seems, which was proved all over again when BR repainted its diesels less than twenty years later. In June 1951 instructions were issued that all blue locomotives were to be painted dark green with black and orange lining. Eventually all thirty were repainted BR Brunswick green and

---

Dimensions, as built.

'The three sets of valve gear...and the inside connecting rod are completely enclosed in an oil bath...lubricated by a circulating oil system, driven by two gear pumps, connected by a chain to the crankshaft.'
Three cylinders: 18in. diameter X 24in. stroke.
Piston valves = 11in..
Bogie wheels = 3ft. 1in. diameter.
Driving wheels = 6ft. 2in. diameter.
Trailing wheels = 3ft. 7in. diameter.
Wheelbase = 6ft. 3in. + 5ft. 6in. + 7ft. 6in. + 7ft. 6in. + 10ft. = 36ft. 9in..

Boiler diameter = 5ft. 9¾in. to 6ft. 3½in.
Boiler length = 16ft. 9½in.
Tube length = 17ft..
Firebox length = 7ft. 10½in..

Heating surfaces
Tubes 124 X 2¼in. = 1,241.6 sq ft.
Flues 40 X 5¼in. = 934.3 sq ft.
Firebox and thermic
syphons = 275 sq ft.
Total evaporative
surface = 2,450.9 sq ft.
Superheater = 665 sq ft.
Total = 3,115.9 sq ft.

Grate area = 48½ sq ft.
Working pressure = 280 lb per sq in.

Tractive effort = 37,500 lb.

Tender = 5 tons of coal and 5,000 gallons of water.
Estimated weight in working order* = Engine 92 tons 10 cwt.
Tender 50 tons 0 cwt.
Total 142 tons 10 cwt.
*As published both by the *Railway Magazine* and *Railway Observer* in 1941. They also published different heating surface figures:-
Tubes   = 1241.6 sq ft.
Flues   = 934.3 sq ft.
Firebox = 275 sq ft.
Total   = 2450.9 sq ft.
Supheat.= 822 sq ft
Total   3272.9 sq ft (*Railway Magazine* gives it as 3,273 sq. ft.)

Rebuilt Dimensions
First one was 35018 BRITISH INDIA LINE. Dealt with at Eastleigh Works between Wednesday 16 November 1955 and Wednesday 14 February 1956. The two main differences were the removal of the air smooth casing and the replacement of the valve gear by conventional Walschaerts arrangement.
Three cylinders = 18in. diameter X 24in. stroke.
Bogie wheels = 3ft. 1in. diameter.
Driving wheels = 6ft. 2in. diameter.
Trailing wheels = 3ft. 7in.
Wheelbase = 6ft. 3in. + 5ft. 6in. + 7ft. 6in.+ 7ft. 6in. + 10ft. = 36ft. 9in.
Length over buffers: As built = 69ft. 7¾in.
           As rebuilt = 71ft. 7¾in.

Heating surfaces:
Tubes and Flues = 2175.9 sq ft.
Firebox = 275sq ft.
Superheater = 612sq ft.
Total = 3062.9sq ft.

Tube length = 17.ft.
Grate area = 48½ sq ft.
Boiler pressure = 250lb.
Tractive Effort = 33,495lb.
NB. Work on reducing the boiler pressure had started in 1952.
Also modernisation of the tenders had started some years before.

35009 was ex-works after rebuilding in March 1957; it was an Exmouth Junction engine and here it is in the shed yard there a few months later, on 15 August 1957. Photograph W. Hermiston, The Transport Treasury.

once again 35024 was the first one dealt with.

Dates to Brunswick green:-
35001 5/52; 35002 6/51; 35003 8/53; 35004 3/53; 35005 2/54; 35006 9/53; 35007 12/52; 35008 5/52; 35009 2/53; 35010 11/52; 35011 11/51; 35012 7/52; 35013 12/52; 35014 8/51; 35015 6/53; 35016 3/53; 35017 4/53; 35018 7/51; 35019 6/51; 35020 6/52; 35021 2/52; 35022 1/52; 35023 3/52; 35024 5/51; 35025 6/52; 35026 6/52; 35027 11/53; 35028 6/53; 35029 7/52; 35030 5/53.

Upon rebuilding, the BR Brunswick green was kept, though the black skirt on the bottom of the cab and tender was left out and rectangular panels appeared instead. These panels also appeared before rebuilding where the engine was paired with a cut-down tender.

How it would end. The 'American' look of the rebuilds encapsulated by 35029 ELLERMAN LINES at Nine Elms, 12 May 1965. Note the speedo; as a general BR policy, these were fitted to all the Merchant Navys from about 1959. Photograph Alec Swain, The Transport Treasury.

The 'original' if that is what we can call 35001 with its vastly altered outline, climbing up out of Blackboy tunnel with the London-bound ACE, with Exmouth Junction concrete depot on the right, 13 August 1954. CHANNEL PACKET itself was among the last of the 'Packets' to be rebuilt, late in 1959 but it is interesting to observe how far it has come to resemble, in small doses, the 'final state' of the original engines. The faring is gone in front of the cylinders, it carries the larger smoke deflectors and it has the wedge cab, though the tender has yet to be 'modified' – that is, cut down; the curves on the casing at the lower edge mark it out as a first series loco. Photograph J. Robertson, The Transport Treasury.

The tender off 21C1 at Eastleigh, No.3111 awaiting attention, 22 September 1945. The tattered canvas sheet has obviously had its day and a length of chain sprocket is dumped on the bulkhead. The mysterious lettering reads: TO BE PUT IN TENDER BEFORE LEAVING SARUM, a reminder to insert water treatment briquettes. The front end filler looks very securely battened down indeed, and hardly likely to give way to a water surge during braking. These first, rather streamlined tenders looked a bit cumbersome on their own but it couldn't have been an easy job to get all those curves right (in such thin metal) and keep them like that. The rear of the cabs curved in to match this curve at the tender's leading edge. (Post-War, the combination of an early Merchant Navy plus Bulleid coaches made for an impressive assembly.) Those long spring hangers went out of use and were not employed on the second batch, though the holes for the brackets that held them were drilled in the frame. Just visible above the notice is a bracket for a wartime 'tin hat'. Photograph H.C. Casserley.

Both looking completely ghastly, 21C2 and 3112, at Salisbury on 20 July 1947. Fire damage might explain the marks on the casing, but the tender just seems to be suffering from extreme weathering, of the sort the blue diesels got in the 1970s. There is a longitudinal patch, recalling the problems when weld lines split under the weight of surging water. Photograph H.C. Casserley.

The Tender Trap

The Merchant Navy tenders abounded in detail variation, a veritable trap for the engine picker. I hope to have outlined the principal changes but in a description the host of minor changes, when and where and how they were effected, will inevitably get blurred or lost, even where one is truly confident of the precise events. With luck, some of these photographs, and others elsewhere in the book, will illustrate most of the points. As you'd expect, the tenders were built in three batches of ten to match the engines, so we have three separate generations, all with their own differences and all sporting the modifications (or not) which might then be applied to pre-existing ones. BR carried on the changes and while doubtless all steam locomotive tenders were effectively re-tanked (and thereby 'rebuilt') over the years

the Merchant Navys have to be one of the few classes where all the tenders had to be *systematically* rebuilt. It is a complex bundle of changes; I hope to have summarised the principal differences at least, enough to set the reader (or perhaps more especially the modeller) on the right path for a particular engine at a particular time. As ever, the right photographs are the best way of avoiding the tender trap...

First Series
The first tenders, for the initial batch of ten engines, 21C1-21C10, were built at Ashford, where apparently the necessary welding techniques and equipment were available. They carried five tons of coal and bore 5,000 gallons of water. These tenders were high at the sides and uncomplicated, the curve at the front of the 'self-trimming' bunker running in line with

the cab roof; at the front the sides ran up and joined to give an arch matching the profile of the cab roof.

The curves at the top of the tender sides, incidentally, are given the curious name 'raves', which apparently dates from the fifteenth century ('origin unknown' according to the *Concise Oxford Dictionary*) and for most of the 600 years or so since has quite innocently referred to the permanent or removable framework added to the sides of carts to increase capacity. The art of engine picking has brought about a modest revival in the fortunes of this otherwise surely doomed word.

On the first two, 21C1 and 21C2, the 'rave' (I just *have* to put that word in inverted commas) ran across the back of the tender to hide the vacuum cylinders and so on that were placed up there. Hidden away inside the tank

The evolution of the Merchant Navy tenders, if it could be summarised, was one of 'destreamlining' and the reduction of frills. Thus the 'raves' gradually disappeared, beginning with the bit at the back (on the first two, the rest didn't have the rear 'raves' to start with) and revealing the vacuum reservoir cylinders, as on 21C11 at Nine Elms in 1946. Note that the 'raves' on the sides had supporting brackets, and that the Bulleid tenders (like many SR tenders in fact) did not carry the traditional cast plate on the rear, to give number, capacity, date and so on. Instead a simple plate giving the number only – 'T3112' or whatever – was attached, barely noticed, to the frames on the left-hand side, under the front steps. Water level on the first two series was determined using an upright pipe with holes in it; when a cock was opened water came out of the relevant hole, each being calibrated to a the nearest thousand gallons or so. The more holes dispensing water, the fuller the tender was. Photograph Collection Alec Swain, The Transport Treasury.

First series tender No.3115 (four steps as opposed to the normal three) behind 35005 CANADIAN PACIFIC (with which it ran most of its life) at Clapham Junction on 13 August 1948. This was the tender fitted with Berkley mechanical stoker (see the earlier section *The Curate's Egg*); the 'raves' do not have the 'depth' of other engines because the tender top has been raised, to compensate for loss of capacity when the stoker gear was installed. Photograph H.C. Casserley.

was a strainer to stop particles (rust flakes, coal fragments, bird feathers and anything else known to man) reaching the injectors. It was an American idea to place this essential item in an accessible place outside, something taken up enthusiastically in the BR Standards where it certainly saved time and labour. Bulleid, like his contemporaries, put the strainers *inside* the tank (there was nothing perverse in this – Stanier's 8Fs were the same for instance) where every inevitable blockage required half a day's stoppage while the tank was drained

and a cleaner lad bullied into climbing inside and clearing the wretched thing. Elsewhere, on post-War LMS locos and on the BR Standards, the strainer was in a box carried on the tender framing, outside. It froze every now and then, true, but blockages and routine maintenance could be settled in minutes. A new strainer later replaced the inside one on the Merchant Navys but even so it was in a sump, behind the framing and still pretty awkward to use.

On the first three tenders the fireman climbed up the back like a monkey, using a complicated

arrangement of footsteps and handrails and doubtless lamp irons too. Like all the tenders, there was a pattern of electric lights for night-time when running backwards – though, as on the LNER, plenty of photographs show traditional lamps stuck on the irons above the electric lights. In any case, locos always had to have a conventional red tail lamp – even the diesels didn't escape this, for some years! Discs were supposed to serve in place of the electric lamps during daylight hours. The familiar tubular steel ladders made their appearance with the fourth tender, fitted to 21C4 CUNARD WHITE STAR. The previous tenders got ladders after a short while. As with many tender attachments, the shape and disposition of the ladders changed over the years.

As a weight saving measure, or possibly because the right material just wasn't to be found in wartime, these first ten tenders had inadequate shells. The metal of the sides was thin (only three sixteenths of an inch) and poorly braced and sometimes just the surging of the full weight of water, let alone a minor yard collision or argument with a fire iron, caused splits or rents in the sheeting. Patches and welds were, literally, 'fingers in the dyke' until some internal rearrangement could be done.

In an attempt to counteract all this, tender 3114 from 21C4 CUNARD WHITE STAR was fitted in January 1944 with additional wash-plates and in April returned to traffic behind 21C7 ABERDEEN & COMMONWEALTH, with noticeable

More 'raves', ladders and liveries, on 35003 ROYAL MAIL at Nine Elms in 1950. The engine is newly in blue, the central rib betraying the asbestos boarding of the casing. First series tender still with long spring hangers, this would be No.3117 originally attached to 21C7 ABERDEEN COMMONWEALTH. Photograph The Transport Treasury.

improvement. When 21C2 UNION CASTLE was in works for its first General Repair (March-June 1944) its tender 3112 in turn had the wash-plates rearranged, together with strengthened side bracing. Many of the welds were redone at the same time, relieving some of the inordinate stresses. This turned out to be the cure, and by December 1945 all ten first series tenders had been similarly modified.

The 'rave' at the rear of the first two tenders was cut away almost to nothing and new ladders with the conspicuous swan necks were fitted, replacing the steps. There were further modifications, rearranging the

deeply unloved and secured more or less permanently, so far as was possible. It is doubtful if they were used much before being quietly done away with after a few years – see their fate later under *Second Series*.

Six of the 5,000-gallon tenders (3113, 3114, 3116, 3118, 3119 and 3120) were partially renewed in 1945-47 but water capacity was not increased or the design modified to that of the second series 5,100 gallon ones. Externally there was no difference, the changes being entirely concerned with the strengthening of the coal space and tank plating, in order to combat rust and rough treatment.

'raves' finally done away with to give those rather pleasingly minimalist edges and slopes with which the engines saw out most of their BR lives and all of their rebuilt lives. 'Modified' is in a way an inappropriate term because it is not that specific, for the Merchant Navy tenders, above all others, perhaps, never stopped getting modified in one way or another. 'Cut down' would be far better in the case of the Merchant Navys but the term 'modified' has, through repeated usage come to mean *only* that – the cutting down of the tenders by BR. So, 'modified' it is.

All thirty Merchant Navy tenders were either cut down (mainly when

Modified first series 5,000 gallon tender on 35004 CUNARD WHITE STAR, late in the day (15 June 1964) at Yeovil shed, keeping unlikely company in the shape of a 64XX pannier tank. The tender would be 3113, originally on 21C3. After 35004 was withdrawn towards the end of 1965 following a furious wheelspin and buckled rods, the tender went to 35029. Photograph The Transport Treasury.

bulkhead at the front with new lockers and forming fire iron tunnels between the 'rave' and the bunker. Windows made for more comfortable tender-first running, though coal debris accumulating in the channel between 'rave' and coal bunker often cancelled out this advantage.

One peculiar feature was a set of two water filling caps at the *front* of the tender. The conventional rear filler remained where it was supposed to be, at the back, and these two front ones were apparently put there for the convenience of the fireman, who wouldn't then have to climb up on the tender back. Unfortunately they could overflow – as any filler could – but into the cab! Or they could burst open as the tender filled from the rear, or merely as water surged forward upon braking. They were, accordingly,

The 'raves' were further reduced under BR, the tenders beginning to acquire the general form with which we all became familiar in the 1950s and 1960s; eight were so dealt with but five were so bad they were rebodied using yet another tank version, 5,250 gallon examples built at Ashford.

****

They rode well and in the later two series offered an unobstructed view rearwards, but the Bulleid tenders were not the lap of luxury; the high sides made watering and coaling hard work. 'Modification' beckoned...

'Modification'
All the Merchant Navy tenders were 'modified' – 'cut down' that is, with the

the locos were rebuilt) or were rebodied – this latter outcome limited to a few rebuilt locos). Cutting down – 'modification' – commenced in 1952 but the programme didn't really get under way until rebuilding of engines started in 1956. To complicate matters a few tenders were first cut down and later still rebodied. The story is best revealed in the individual engine and tender pairings

Vacuum Cylinders
If the ladders, steps and fillers and just about everything else on a Merchant Navy tender changed and migrated during the working lives of the locomotives, the most prominent feature to change was the vacuum cylinder arrangement. They could be found in almost every possible configuration over the years, whether

Modified third series tender, No.3349 which had been with 35027 since new, near Clapham on 3 June 1963. Cab curve dented with years of Nine Elms and Exmouth Junction's coalers; note partially covered vacuum cylinders (you can see how terribly vulnerable those connecting pipes were with big lumps of coal falling about – or even a fireman's boots), briquette hatch and single round water filler cap. Photograph J.G. Walmsley, The Transport Treasury.

covered or uncovered. Strictly speaking, they were the vacuum reservoir cylinders; interconnected by piping, there were three of them, set atop the tender and slightly off centre, held together by metal bands. They were set differently (of course) on other tenders – on some 6,000 gallon ones for instance, there were two one side and one on the other. Like this, they proved vulnerable to damage by falling lumps when taking coal. When the BR briquette system of water treatment came in there was more 'room on top' and the vacuum cylinders were repositioned more close in behind the bunker and all were covered over in one way or another.

Second Series
The second series of Merchant Navys, 21C11-21C20, naturally got a separate tender design from the first series. This time they held 5,100 gallons. Ladders were remodelled while the appearance was rather different – this was because the top edge of the sides ran straight all the length of the tender body. They still had the front fillers and the 'tunnels' between the 'raves' and the bunker sides had hinged lights for forward running.

The long spring hangers of the earlier first series 5,000 gallon tenders were replaced by brackets on the spring ends; this modification was determined upon after Ashford began assembly and the unplugged holes for the hangers remained as evidence of

this late change of mind – see photographs and occasional comments, mainly in the individual photographs in *The Record*. The steam carriage-heating pipe was now visible (very much so – again, prominent in many photographs) below the tank instead of being concealed behind the skirt of the tender side.

Water surges from the front fillers when braking hard remained a problem but the idea of these things had happily lost support at court; the last three, 21C18, 21C19 and 21C20, went into service with the fillers plated over and the others, 21C1-21C17, were so treated fairly quickly, by 1946. Bradley records that much of this work was actually done at the sheds even before authorisation was officially issued. The sheds were obviously anxious, where they could, to do away with this particular mortification as soon as possible!

(Although Second Series capacity was officially given as five tons of coal and 5,100 gallons of water, a test in March 1945 revealed these to be six tons and 5,194 gallons.)

Modification
When the second series tenders were modified the top edge of the bunker was revealed to have an inward curve to it; moreover the vacuum cylinders were fully enclosed, the position of the TIA tank varied and later on a smaller cover for the vacuum cylinders appeared.

Third Series
The last ten 'BR' Merchant Navys, 35021-35030, saw the introduction of a third major tender variant – 6,000 gallon vehicles, six wheeled as before but with an unequal wheelbase of 7ft. 4in. by 7ft. (total wheelbase 14ft. 4in.); this compared with 6ft. 6in. + 6ft. 6in. (13ft. total) on the first twenty. The increase in capacity was reportedly to alleviate crews' fears of running dry on non-stop Waterloo-Bournemouth jobs. The new tenders looked similar to their predecessors but by now of course the front filler holes had gone. The ladders were different again, so were the vacuum cylinders; the important variation was TIA.

Traitement Integral Armand represented the sort of water treatment that the steel fireboxes should have got from the first (upon which the success of such boxes in America was predicated) and it was extended to all the other twenty Merchant Navys by 1951. It had been standard fare on the SNCF for years and was far more 'scientific' than most procedures familiar at running sheds, requiring some firm adherence to daily schedules of upkeep. Water in the tender and boiler was tested chemically during an engine's daily work and water, charged with the treatment solution at appropriate strength, was discharged automatically from a small tank set on the top of the tender behind the bunker. The composition of this solution was supposed to vary according to the volume of water going into the tank, from day to day according to the results of daily examinations. Doubtless in the 'front line' reality of everyday working it was rather less perfectly carried out than this.

The result was that the scale-forming compounds in hard water were precipitated out as a soft mud, eliminating the hardness of the water and stopping corrosion. A blowdown valve operated from the cab every half an hour or so of running blew out the sludge and deposited it on the track to either soak or wash away, or dry out and blow away in the breeze. The system famously increased boiler wash-out periods from seven to *fifty-six* days, happily coinciding with the inspection period for the firebox stays and plates.

A correspondent for *The Railway Observer* was around at Eastleigh when the final batch of Merchant Navys was being built and in the cabs of 35021-35025 he reported, there was *'a gauge and clock combined which is made by ACFI and calibrated in French lettering with the face of the dial marked off in days, Lundi, Mardi etc. 35027 does not appear to have these cab fittings whilst 35026 has not been checked. 34033 a 'West Country', now carrying tender No.3286 was ex-works week ending 11.12.48 and also has these cab and tender fittings'.*

The simpler and cheaper BR system of briquettes replaced the TIA apparatus from about 1956. A simple tube replaced the tender top mixing

tank, its presence indicate only by a small filler cap, looking like a smaller version of the main filler. Briquettes were loaded in the shute below the cap every few days and like the TIA system, adjusted according to the results of regular water analyses. A small yellow circle on the cabside below the number indicated TIA, and later a yellow triangle was applied to show that the BR water treatment was installed instead.

There was a further complication with the third series in that Brighton Works, which this time had got the job of making the tenders, failed to have enough ready in time. This meant that five of the new Merchant Navys came out with spare light Pacific tenders. 35021, 35022 and 35024 came out with 5,500 gallon Battle of Britain tenders and 35026 and 35027 with 4,500 gallon West Country tenders. All got their proper 6,000 gallon tenders within a few months as they became ready; one BB tender, No.3333, was passed from one Merchant Navy, 35021, straight to another, 35024, before going on to its proper 'intended'.

Modification
The third series, 6,000 gallon tenders were modified like the rest; the 6,000 gallon example No.3342, attached to 35021 NEW ZEALAND LINE, was indeed the first. The bunker top edge also had a curve to it. The bunker was not as long as on the two earlier series and there was much more room on top for the various items; the vacuum cylinders were partly covered in.

'New BR Bodies'
Five of the first series 5,000 gallon tenders were rebuilt over the period 1959-1963. 5,250 gallon tanks (they were later found to hold fifty or so gallons more than this) with entirely new tops were made at Ashford and fitted to tenders which had suffered particularly badly from corrosion. These were (as given in Bradley):

3111	(35001)	2/63
3112	(35002)	4/60
3115	(35005)	5/59
3117	(35003)	8/59
3118	(35018)	1/62

No.3343, the ex-coal weighing tender, was also re-bodied, as from February 1962, but its capacity was 6,000 gallons. All rebodied tenders were readily identifiable by their straight profile tops

The Coal Weighing Tender
This was No.3343, a standard third series 6,000 gallon tender modified by replacing the top parts in 1952. The main apparatus weighed the coal put into the bunker (which became a sort of separate weighing table) and readings were made and set from equipment in a padlocked cabinet at the rear of the bunker. (Even this minor detail, of course, changed over the years.) Like some of those on the other Regions the SR's coal-weighing tender rode around for years serving in a conventional fashion with the weighing bunker firmly secured (as it always was when running) and the equipment probably rusted solid, until the thing was dismantled and the

35021 NEW ZEALAND LINE restarts after a signal check at Basingstoke, 4 August 1964. Another modified third series 6,000 gallon tender, No.3342 (now running with CLAN LINE) subtly different from its sister 3349 behind 35027 in the previous photograph; cab curve cut back (probably damaged) different vacuum pipework, prominent 'spout' and different site for briquette hatch. The 'spout' is an air vent (not all tenders had them and the position varied when they did – naturally!) and was not the 'breather' pipe desirable on tenders which took water from troughs, there being of course, no troughs on the SR. Photograph Alec Swain, The Transport Treasury.

Tender 3115 again, still with 35005 CANADIAN PACIFIC (running into Waterloo with a late afternoon train, 14 May 1965) and still with the frames seen earlier at Nine Elms but now with the first of the Ashford-fabricated 5,250 gallon bodies to go to a Merchant Navy (some had gone to light Pacifics), fitted in May 1959. It has a single, 'central' (actually offset) ladder, covered vacuum tanks and rectangular filler lids (one each side) with the BR briquette shute between them. The water filler caps (various types, size and number), BR briquette shute/holder, TIA tank, vacuum cylinders and ladders together have, potentially, an almost limitless variety of combinations. It doesn't make it easy... In the background, incidentally, is the old Waterloo training school. Photograph Peter Groom.

tender rebodied in 1962, as noted above.

Mark Arscott of Markits ('all your 4mm Bulleid wheel needs' 01923 249711) writes: 'It entered traffic on 11 June 1952 attached to 35018, regularly rostered by Nine Elms to the 10.30am Waterloo-Bournemouth. It was back in the works 28 September 1952, where it was removed and after adjustments to the drawgear and springing and minor modifications to the weighing equipment, on 8 November 1952 was attached to 35014. This locomotive carried the boiler (No.1107) without the thermic syphons and was of particular interest to the trials staff. It was worked extensively on Bournemouth and West of England expresses and Nine Elms-Southampton fitted freights. After these trials, the tender remained with 35014 until the loco entered Eastleigh for rebuilding on 18 May 1956. The tender reappeared in July 1956 attached to 35015; was removed on 1 May 1958 and from 14 May that year was attached to 35024. The pair entered Eastleigh Works and re-emerged with 35024 now rebuilt, the tender remaining attached until 20 December 1961, when the coal weighing equipment was removed and the tender rebodied with a stretched version of the 5,250 gallon tank – which would have held considerably more than 6,000 gallons. It was then partnered with 35008, in February 1962. In October 1964 it was withdrawn and sent to Woodhams in South Wales for scrap, attached to 35018. Despite this, 3343 is still with us today, with its last partner 35018.'

The Tender Tale

21C1/35001: no.3111 2/41; no.3112 5/41 (while no.3111 received tank welding and axle box repairs), no.3111 5/41 (modified 6/56); rebodied 2/63; no.3349 3/65 (after engine withdrawn).

21C2/35002: no.3112 6/41; no.3115 3/52; no.3112 3/52 (modified 5/58); rebodied 4/60.
21C3/35003: no.3113 9/41; no.3117 2/44 (rebodied 8/59).
21C4/35004: no.3114 10/41(modified 9/56); no.3113 1/44 (modified 6/58), no.3121 10/65.
21C5/35005: no.3115 12/41 (rebodied 5/59); no.3348 8/65.
21C6/35006: no.3116 12/41 – stayed with 35006 all its working life. Modified 8/59.
21C7/35007: no.3117 6/42; no.3114 5/44 (modified 9/56); no.3127 9/66.
21C8/35008: no.3118 6/42 (modified 5/57); no.3343 2/62; no.3118 10/64.
21C9/35009: no.3119 6/42 – stayed with 35009 all its working life. Modified 3/57.
21C10/35010: no.3120 7/42 (modified 1/57); no.3122 12/64, fitted at Nine Elms.
21C11/35011: no.3121 12/44 (modified 8/57); no.3129 10/65.
21C12/35012: no.3122 1/45 (modified 7/52); no.3343 7/52 for 2 weeks supposedly; may well not be 'real'; no. 3122 7/52; no. 3120 12/64.
21C13/35013: no.3123 2/45; no.3124 8/50 (modified 12/52).
21C14/35014: no.3124 2/45; no.3123 6/50; no.3343 11/52; no.3126 7/56; no.3345 3/65; no.3115 9/65.
21C15/35015: no.3126 (modified 7/56); no.3343 7/56; no.3123 (modified 6/58).
21C16/35016: no.3125 3/45 – stayed with 35016 all its working life. Modified 4/57.
21C17/35017: no.3127 4/45; LMS no.10123 4/48; no.3127 6/48 (modified 3/57); no.3114 9/66 (after engine withdrawn.)
21C18/35018: no.3129 5/45; no.3343 7/52; no.3346 10/52 (modified 2/56); no.3118 (rebodied 1/62); no.3343 10/64 (after engine withdrawn).
21C19/35019: no.3128 6/45; LMS no.10219 4/48; no.3128 5/48 (modified 5/59).
21C20/35020: no.3130 7/45; LMS no.10373 5/48; no.3130 6/48; no.3347 6/52 (modified 6/53); no.3345 5/56 (for tests on Swindon Plant); no.3344 7/56.
35021: no.3333 9/48 (BB tender, 5,500 gallons); no.3342 11/48 (modified 2/52); no.3126 10/65 (after engine withdrawn).
35022: no.3335 10/48 (BB tender, 5,500 gallons); no.3345 1/49; no.3347 6/56.
35023: no.3341 11/48 – stayed with 35023 all its working life; modified 2/57.
35024: no.3333 11/48 (BB tender, 5,500

Below. Second series 5,100 gallon tender No.3125, behind 35016 ELDERS FYFFES at Nine Elms about August 1957, shortly after it was modified. The vacuum tanks were entirely enclosed, in two or three ways (naturally) and some covers were bigger than others. A further variation could came into play so far as the TIA tank was concerned – said mixing tank projects out from under the main vacuum cylinder cover. Photograph J. Robertson, The Transport Treasury.

gallons); no.3346 2/49; no.3123 11/52; no.3343 5/58; no.3346 12/61.

35025: no.3343 11/48; no.3350 6/52 (modified 12/56).

35026: no.3260 12/48 (WC tender, 4,500 gallons); no.3350 7/49; no.3130 6/52 (modified 1/57); no.3349 3/65; no.3111 4/65.

35027: no.3288 12/48 (WC tender, 4,500 gallons); no.3349 4/49 (modified 5/57); no.3130 3/65.

35028: no.3344 12/48 (modified 7/56); no.3345 7/56 (modified 10/59); no.3126 3/65; no.3342 10/65.

35029: no.3347 2/49; no.3129 7/52 (modified 9/59); no.3113 10/65.

35030: no.3348 4/49 (modified 4/58); no.3345 10/65.

'*Rebodied*' *indicates the need for a new tank where corrosion had worn the original out – were 5,250 gallons and retained the five tons coal capacity, except that rebodied tender 3343 was 6,000 gallons.*

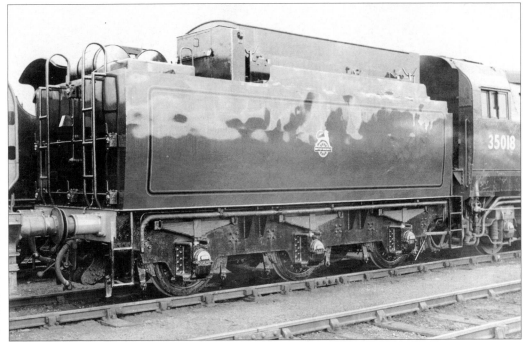

Above. The coal-weighing tender, looking a bit wrinkled but virtually newly modified behind 35018 at Eastleigh on 12 July 1952; it's useful among other things for an unusual view of the sanding pipe on the tender (the straight narrow pipe pointing at the leading tender wheel). Some of the weighing gear (or more accurately perhaps the gear for fixing it down when running) can be seen 'on top' together with the padlocked control cabinet. It has 'Lord Nelson' vacuum tanks mounted cross-wise, a TIA box and as yet does not have any tender cab roofing. The unions objected to its absence and the tender could not be used until one was fitted. A clash in lining is revealed – the tender is panelled but the cab remains straight lined, to match a high-sided tender. Photograph Les Elsey.

1975 was a distant prospect indeed. 35005 CANADIAN PACIFIC in the shed yard at Eastleigh on 28 July 1959, a matter of days out of the works after rebuilding, running in no doubt complete and ready to work to its home shed Nine Elms. A sparkling, quite beautiful sight. The tender has been rebodied and now has a capacity of 5,250 gallons. Note 8P and circle on cab, sandboxes with conventional filler caps and Wakefield lubricators. Photograph Les Elsey.

A Long Way Short of 1975

The Southern Regional Accountant was sadly adrift in his calculations concerning the longevity of the Merchant Navys. If he had been right they would have still been in and out of Waterloo in 1975 and with a bit of luck circumstances might have contrived to see some survivors working a remnant steam service in – 1980? It is fanciful stuff, and probably a wicked accounting ploy in any case, a shameless device to enhance the case for rebuilding. What would all these surviving Pacifics (converted to oil?) have done anyway? The scenario demands at least a long-postponed Bournemouth electrification… Well, we can dream.

The 1958 allocation, with most of the Merchant Navys rebuilt, was:
70A Nine Elms: 35005, 35012, 35014, 35016, 35017, 35018, 35019, 35020, 35029, 35030.
71B Bournemouth: 35010, 35021, 35022, 35025, 35026, 35027.
72A Exmouth Jct: 35002, 35003, 35008, 35009, 35011, 35013, 35023, 35024.
72B Salisbury: 35004, 35006, 35007.
73A Stewarts Lane: 35001, 35015, 35028.

For a period Eastleigh Works concentrated on the rebuilding of some of the light Pacifics (the first one was 34005 BARNSTAPLE); 35015 ROTTERDAM LLOYD was rebuilt in the summer of 1958 and became the first of the class (often photographed at the head of the 'Golden Arrow') to run on the Eastern Section 'in modified form'. The term, widely used at the time, hardly *seemed* to do justice to the transmogrification which was achieved but this was largely a visual effect. We should not lose sight of the fact, for instance, that Jarvis himself was proud of retaining 85% of the original…

By 1961 the Kent Coast Electrification saw the allocation concentrated westwards:
70A Nine Elms: 35001, 35012, 35014, 35015, 35016, 35017, 35019, 35020, 35028, 35029, 35030
71B Bournemouth: 35002, 35005, 35008, 35011, 35018, 35021, 35023, 35024, 35027.
72A Exmouth Junction: 35003, 35009, 35010 (high speed slip – broken cylinder casting), 35013, 35022, 35025, 35026.
72B Salisbury: 35004, 35006, 35007.

Only one other shed received an allocation of the class after 1961, the one-time GWR establishment at Weymouth which had come under the Southern's wing in 1958. The WR took over Exmouth Junction recoded 83D from September 1963 and its Pacifics became WR stock; they carried on with the London jobs and still received maintenance at Eastleigh Works. In 1964 General Repairs were abandoned and from then on the engines had a fixed, and limited, lifetime. That year saw the first withdrawals: 35002 and 35015 in January 1964, 35018 and 35006, both in August, 35009 and 35025 in September, 35001 in November.

Increasing numbers of redundant steam locomotives meant British Railways did not have the capacity to scrap them all, indeed 35020 BIBBY LINE was the only one of the class cut up by BR, at Eastleigh Works in March 1965. It might have been dismal for the enthusiast but was certainly a 'golden age' for the British scrapman, though there were some little bits of temporary relief. On 11 January 1964 for instance 35003 ROYAL MAIL was noted at Eastleigh Works marked for scrap, but 'had now returned to service after overhaul and is at Exmouth Junction'. It was in works from 13/1-25/1/64 for a light casual repair and remained in service right to the end of Southern steam, in July 1967.

Withdrawals in 1965 were 35004 (high speed slip; broken cylinder casting, cut-up by Cohens in Eastleigh shed), 35005, 35016, 35019, 35020, 35021 and 35024. This left sixteen in service by the end of the year and the survivors worked on the last main line steam passenger workings over the next couple of years. It was a curious period when rundown, cannibalisation and sometimes abject failure marched side by side with some of the finest performances seen as some crews resolved to rise above it all. There were sights on which you'd have got very long odds a few years before – on 23 January 1965 45674 DUNCAN, an *officially withdrawn* Crewe North Jubilee of all things, worked into Bournemouth on a parcels train from Crewe and later piloted 35030 ELDER DEMPSTER LINES on to Weymouth with the down 'Royal Wessex.' Short of comets in the sky, plagues of frogs and so on, this was rum stuff.

1966 was the last full year of steam operation on the former LSWR main line to Bournemouth and by the end of the year the following had gone: 35010, 35011, 35017, 35022, 35027 and 35029. Dieselisation on the London-Salisbury workings had reduced their sphere of operations still further; allocations on 1 January 1966 were:
Bournemouth: 35003, 35008, 35010, 35011, 35013, 35023 and 35027.
Weymouth: 35007, 35012, 35014, 35017, 35022, 35026, 35028, 35029 and 35030.

Nine Elms was, strangely, reduced to little more than a servicing point so far as Merchant Navys were concerned, but there was something of a comeback later – see below.

By now the survivors were often running in poor external condition, in some cases without nameplates or smokebox numberplates. From now until the end of Southern steam further transfers did take place and for a while Nine Elms once again had an allocation of Merchant Navys, though Bournemouth lost its complement.

Transfers in 1966 and 1967:-
35003 October 1966 to 70G; February 1967 to 70A; xd 7/67.
35007 February 1967 to 70A; xd 7/67.
35008 October 1966 to 70G; February 1967 to 70A; xd 7/67.
35010 xd 9/66 from 70F.
35011 xd 2/66 from 70F .
35012 February 1967 to 70A; xd 4/67.
35013 October 1966 to 70G; February 1967 to 70A; xd 7/67.
35014 xd 4/67 from 70G.
35017 xd 7/66 from 70G .
35022 xd 6/66 from 70G .
35023 October 1966 to 70G; February 1967 to 70A; xd 7/67.
35026 xd 4/67 from 70G.
35027 xd 10/66 from 70F.
35028 February 1967 to 70A; xd 7/67.
35029 xd 9/66 from 70G.
35030 February 1967 to 70A; xd 7/67.
xd = withdrawn; 70A = Nine Elms; 70F = Bournemouth; 70G = Weymouth.

At the end of July 1967 Nine Elms still held 35007, 35008, 35012, 35013, 35023, 35028 and 35030; 35003, 35024 and 35026 were dumped at Weymouth and they were all gradually 'staged' west to South Wales for scrap, usually involving a stop-over in the dead Salisbury shed yard. The last engines to leave there for the South Wales scrapyards were 34102 LAPFORD, 35023 HOLLAND-AFRIKA LINE and 34034 HONITON, hauled away by Hymek D7045 with all three steam locomotives cut up at Buttigiegs, Newport.

What about today's survivors?
35005 CANADIAN PACIFIC, currently in non-authentic BR Blue, is successfully negotiating the main line.
35006 PENINSULA & ORIENTAL S.N. Co. Gloucester & Warwickshire Railway undergoing restoration.
35009 SHAW SAVILL awaiting restoration on the Mid-Hants Railway.
35010 BLUE STAR LINE under restoration on Colne Valley Railway, Essex.
35011 GENERAL STEAM NAVIGATION currently undergoing restoration on the Swanage Railway.
35018 BRITISH INDIA LINE currently undergoing restoration on the Mid-Hants Railway.
35022 HOLLAND-AMERICA LINE awaiting restoration on the Swanage Railway. (Is talk of returning it to an original).
35025 BROCKLEBANK LINE awaiting restoration on the Swanage Railway.
35027 PORT LINE currently steaming up and down the Swanage Railway.
35028 CLAN LINE (now air-braked) was purchased directly from BR along with 34023 and never saw a scrap yard. Today spends much of its time hauling the UK part of the Orient Express.
35029 ELLERMAN LINES sectioned in National Railway Museum, York.

Splendidly, luxuriantly, scintillatingly finished, the first Bulleid Pacific, the original 'Packet', glints in the sun alongside the Eastleigh coal stage on 10 November 1962 with rebodied tender. Its condition seems to owe nothing to any recent repair, it is just in perfect external nick. This was not the first time it had appeared radiant – for sheer splendour, for instance, its highly polished appearance in April 1946 for the reintroduced 'Golden Arrow' took some beating. Notice the screw reverse set in a recess in the firebox side, replacing the troublesome steam reverser and the BR speedo, as well as the phenomenon known as 'pockets'. They are difficult to see and describe. The lengthened valve spindles (1959) extended forward and holes were cut ahead of them in the sloping footplating. These holes had to be covered by the said 'pockets' which, inevitably with this class, were of no less than three different types. The covers came to double as footsteps, beginning life (on 35022 only) as cone shapes *inside* the smoke deflectors, progressing to boxes and finally, as seen here, becoming larger boxes *either side of* the smoke deflector, which had to be cut round them. Once you get your eye in they are quite plain in views such as these but I admit, it took a while even to believe in them! Follow your eye leftwards from the top edge of the AWS battery box (35001 was the first to get AWS incidentally) and stop after about two feet... The wheel in the firebox 'shoulder', often prominent in photographs of the rebuilt engines, is the steam manifold cock. Photograph Les Elsey.

NOTES ACCOMPANYING TABLES

Works: 1

Works visits in this section are calculated partly from *Railway Observer* reports, married to such details as there are on the Record Cards (not all of which exist in their entirety). These refer to a four week period in which the engine was taken in, say 23/1/42-22/2/42, 22/9/47-19/11/47 and so on. In the tables *Works: 1*, only the first date (e.g. 23/1/42, 22/9/47) is given. Dates for certain other work relate to the *end* of a works period, however, so the two are often not strictly comparable; boiler changes for instance are given at the end of a period but the two are easy to match up. Take 21C6; its boiler change to 1093 of 9/46 relates to the *Works:1* date of 15/7/46. It was back in works 13/9/48 and that would be when it got its third boiler, 1111.

Works: 2

The Works record in BR days has been reconstructed from copies of relevant forms (BR9215 in the main) kept at the National Railway Museum at York and the Public Record Office at Kew, along with the form BR9637 *British Railways Southern Region Return of locomotives undergoing or awaiting repairs at Eastleigh Works*, kept at Kew. BR9637 is only available between January 1954 and January 1965. For much of the BR period the same shopping forms were used at Ashford, Brighton Eastleigh and even Ryde Works, completed in triplicate when each locomotive left after repair. One card was to be retained at the works and the other two sent to the Motive Power Superintendent's Head Office. In the case of a locomotive being repaired at Brighton certain information might need to be obtained from Ashford or Eastleigh.

This record allows us to show the period actually in works – 'in/out' as it were – and this is reproduced accordingly, along with certain mileages and the level of repair:

LI Light Intermediate
HI Heavy Intermediate
LC Light Casual
HC Heavy Casual
GO General Overhaul
NC Non Classified

Some were upgraded as the work unfolded, which explains such entries as **LI-GO**. Very rarely it was downgraded, e.g. **LC-NC**. Mileages given in *Works: 2* = 'since last General' 'Works' always means Eastleigh unless noted otherwise.

w/e = week ending

p/e = period ending (invariably four weeks)

There was a general breakdown of record keeping at the end of steam so figures for years such as 1966 and 1967 can have unexpected gaps.

The Record Cards describe very many 'Tests' which relate to jobs done; these are recorded simply by a reference number. Here is a list of 'Tests', in no set order, an illustration (merely) of

A mist-shrouded ROYAL MAIL, in green by now, about 1955. The casing ahead of the cylinder has been removed. Close up, in this sort of unforgiving light, the casing can seem rather less 'air-smoothed' than its designer might fondly have imagined. The A4s and Coronations could look the same – those sweeping smooth curves could dissolve into a mass of joins and rivets, in the right (or wrong) light. Photograph The Transport Treasury.

something of the breadth and complexity of the task while 'in works'. No special significance should be attached to the title under each number – they seemed to vary over time and their accuracy as entries is not guaranteed for each Record Card. This should be regarded as a 'flavour' of the work only – 'new floorboards' are understandable enough but just what was 'Metcalfe's steam heat couplings (new test)' for instance? Such work was recorded as 'U' ('Undisturbed'), or 'R' ('Reconditioned') or sometimes ('Overhauled').

1954:
2204   LMR steam heat relief valve.
2195   Self cleaning smokebox gear (revised test).
2242   Coupling rods MN class (new test).
2081   Regulator valve seating.
2196   Modified steam reverser.
2231   Tender raves and tool pockets.

2219   Single blastpipe and chimney (35019 works visit 18/2/54-27/2/54)

1958:
2207   Drain pipe fitted to tender TIA doser tank.
2300   Modified whistle valve springs.

1959:
2296   Bogie and coupled springs (new test).

1960:
2304   Inside big end cotters.
2310   Eccentric strap bolts and locking plates.
2322   Inside cylinder lubrication.
2321   Sand ejector steam nozzles.
2319   TIA blowdown valve type C.
2302   Inside big end heat detector.
2305   Driving coupling rod bushes.
2282   Boiler water gauge and drain cocks.
2307   Mechanical lubricator drive.

2304   MN and WC inside big end cotters (new test).
2285   Metcalfe's steam heat couplings (new test).

1961:
2341   New floorboards to drawing E52266 (new).

Below. **35001 had a couple of brief spells on the Eastern Section; this is during its second stint, passing Shakespeare Halt (the tender was modified in 1956) on 5 August 1957. Traditionally there were three Merchant Navys at Stewarts Lane, supposedly for the boat trains for which they had been so heroically squeezed into the restrictive profile all those years before. However, they lived a quiet life compared to the majority of their fellows over on the Western Section; Bradley for instance (*Locomotives of the Southern Railway Part Two*, RCTS, 1976) reckoned that, holiday times aside they 'seldom earned their keep'. Photograph J. Robertson, The Transport Treasury.**

21C1 CHANNEL PACKET

Entered service 5 June 1941 part of order No.1068.
Named 10/3/41 in Eastleigh Works Yard by Rt. Hon. J.T.C. Moore-Brabazon, Minister of Transport.

From new fitted with cast gunmetal cabside number plates and sloping number plate above the buffer beam which was later re-affixed on a vertical face. On the tender side were cast SOUTHERN plates, also on the smokebox door in an inverted horseshoe shape – replaced in early 1942 by a full circular type. For a while in May 1942 it was fitted with tender 3112 while the original 3111 received repairs.

Renumbered 35001 10/49; it lost its smokebox door roundel and cast plates but received a smokebox number plate as 35001.

For Tenders and Liveries - see separate Sections.

Allocations
Salisbury p/e 5/6/41
Exmouth Jct. autumn 1942
Stewarts Lane 4/46*
Exmouth Jct. 4/46
Stewarts Lane p/e 25/1/57
Nine Elms p/e 14/6/59
Bournemouth p/e 14/9/64
*short term loan to cover
reintroduced Golden Arrow

Boilers
1090
1102 8/47
1115 12/50

Works: 1

24/6/41	*Left works 22/8/41.*
18/12/41	*Fitted with new valve gear chains and modified oil bath, having covered 11,069 miles since 4/6/41.*
18/5/42	
23/9/42	*New right hand side cylinder.*
26/8/43	*Smokebox hood fitted.*
13/7/44	*General Overhaul 89,995 miles*
20/8/45	*Left works 3/12/45. New cylinders, speedo, 143,639 miles.*
21/3/46	*Ex-works 9/4/46. Fittings for Golden Arrow regalia.*
11/48	*Exmouth Junction repair.*
22/8/49	*Renumbered, BR blue livery.*
22/5/50	*Left works 24/6/50 attention to tyres on driving wheels.*
27/10/50	*Ex-works w/e 4/11/50; repaint and checkover to work special train for Queen of the Netherlands.*
20/11/50	*Ex-works 30/12/50 with V-fronted cab.*
17/3/52	

Works: 2
(Mileages = since last General Overhaul)

15/4/52-w/e 17/5/52**I**		
14/5/53-16/5/53**NC**	*Axle examined for flaws.*	
4/6/53-11/6/53**LC**	*Driving axle replaced.*	
29/9/53-30/10/53**LI**		
7/12/53-10/12/53	*'Return' for previous LI.*	
11/6/54-12/6/54**NC**	*257,240 miles.*	
17/2/55-12/3/55**LI**	*292,480 miles. Three modifications, boiler pressure reduced.*	
30/4/56-9/6/56**GO**	*361,312 miles. Eleven modifications, safety valves resited.*	
12/11/57-7/12/57**LI**	*82,942 miles. One modification, 'Test 2207', 'drain pipe and clip for Tender TIA Doser Tank'.*	
27/5/59-8/8/59**GO**	*126,394 miles. BR type AWS fitted. Rebuilt having covered 807,318 miles since new.*	
8/12/60-14/1/61**LC-HI**	*83,669 miles. Repair upgraded to HI. Speedo fitted and briquette tube feeder added.*	
3/1/63-2/2/63**LI**	*198,007 miles. New tender tank, 5,250 gallons.*	
27/11/63-28/12/63**LC**	*243,516 miles.*	

Withdrawn 22/11/64 having worked 1,095,884 miles; stored at Eastleigh shed 12/64-2/65. Sold with tender 3349 to Birds, Morriston, Swansea and scrapped there by April, 1965.

CHANNEL PACKET in the mid-1950s at its then home shed, Exmouth Junction; tender still with black-out slides. The engine, fully coaled up, is on the shed's exit roads (that's the concrete depot on the right) and will be ready to back down to Exeter for an up working, namely the ACE. Photograph W. Hermiston, The Transport Treasury.

21C2 UNION CASTLE

Entered traffic 16 June 1941, part of order No.1068.

Named on 4/7/41 at Platform 7, Victoria Station by Mr R.F. Gibb, director of the shipping line. From new had cast plates like 21C1.

Worked down Salisbury-Southampton goods trains 5-10/6/41; Salisbury-Eastleigh goods trains 20-23/8/41 and the 'Early morning goods from Salisbury-Southampton 25/8/41'. On 13 August 1945, Stewarts Lane footplate crews worked 21C2 on the 8.55am Victoria-Ramsgate to familarise themselves with the engine, and on 15-17August the engine had test runs Victoria to Dover Marine, two return trips each day with ten Pullmans and two corridor coaches.

Renumbered 35002 in January, 1950.

For Tenders and Liveries - see separate Sections.

Allocations
Salisbury 16/6/41
Exmouth Jct. autumn 1942
Bournemouth p/e 13/5/54
Exmouth Jct. p/e 22/6/54
Bournemouth 6/6/58
Nine Elms p/e 24/11/60
Bournemouth p/e 17/1/61
Nine Elms p/e 27/1/64

Boilers
1091
1096 11/47
1090 11/50
1121 9/54
1114 11/58

Works: 1

24/6/41	*Left 19/8/41*
27/1/42	*Attention to main steampipes having run 15,411 miles.*
22/6/42	
18/3/44	*First General Repair. Smokebox hood; 97,212 miles.*
19/3/45	*Ex-works 10/7/45, fitted with a speed recorder and three new cylinders. 139,675 miles.*
21/5/46	*Noted on works 9/6/46 with the Flaman speed recorder disconnected.*
4/10/47	
Jan. 1949	*Heavy Intermediate at Exmouth Jct. having run 67,254 miles.*
22/8/49	
20/10/49	*Ex-works w/e 7/1/50.*
21/5/51	*Repainted green.*

Works: 2
(Mileages = since last General Overhaul)

3/7/52-22/8/52	**I**	
13/5/53-15/5/53	**NC**	*Axle examined for flaws only.*
1/12/53-31/12/53	**LI**	*Cab modified.*
1/6/54-5/6/54	**NC**	*226,358 miles. 'Modification 176, Test 2242'.*
8/9/54-22/9/54	**NC**	*249,330 miles. Boiler pressure reduced.*
8/7/55-27/8/55	**GO**	*274,531 miles. Twelve modifications, 'Tests 2268 2274 and Intermediate type crank axle fitted'. Safety valves resited.*
7/3/56-21/4/56	**LC**	*(Bricklayers Arms shop)*
30/8/56-22/9/56	**LI-HI**	*60,136 miles. Seven modifications, 'Tests 2268 and 2274'.*
21/6/57-29/6/57	**NC**	*122,816 miles. Tests 2268 and 2274.*
28/3/58-10/5/58	**GO**	*161,982 miles. Ten modifications, 'Tests 2264, 2277, 2081 and 2289. Rebuilt having run 776,797 miles, tender rebodied to 5,250 gallons.*
30/5/58-20/6/58	**NC**	*162,850 miles. 'Tests 2264, 2277, 2081 and 2289.*
12/11/59-9/12/59	**LC**	*Repair at Exmouth Junction.*
22/3/60-9/4/60	**LI**	*117,837 miles. AWS and speedo fitted.*
5/9/61-22/11/61	**LC**	*(Bricklayers Arms shop)*
27/9/62-3/11/62	**LI**	*275,140 miles.*

Withdrawn February 1964 having run 1,101,194 miles, stored at Nine Elms shed January-July 1964 and scrapped at Slag Reduction Co. Rotherham, December, 1964.

UNION CASTLE unclothed, standing in the yard at Nine Elms in 1962. No speedo, pre-AWS, the three sand filling points replicating the sites in the old casing; sanding on the original engines had (eventually) been to the front of all three coupled wheels but, as we know, the leading one had been blanked off because of the problem of sand getting on the slidebars. In the rebuilds the leading sander was restored; the middle sander served the front of the middle driver as before but the rear one, instead of supplying the rear wheel, was turned round to deliver to the rear of the middle driver, for running in reverse. The rebuilt locomotives are often assumed to have been superior to their predecessors in almost every way but as this book tries to demonstrate, this was not the whole case by any means. Just as Bulleid paid for advantages in disadvantages (as any engineering undertaking does) so it was with the rebuilds. The old oil bath was difficult and dirty to work on but that isn't really the point; it was *intended* to be relatively maintenance free and, for much of the time it was. It's great drawback lay in the fact that when it *did* need attention the job was usually horrible. But look at the successor; in the rebuilt engines there was very little space indeed between the frames; most of the time the originals didn't need a pit but with the new engines one was essential – just look at the tiny gap between the wheels, made worse by the brake gear. Getting in there was not fun, by any means. Photograph The Transport Treasury.

**35003 ROYAL MAIL in blue at Andover with a train, 21 June 1950. In blue livery with black 'skirt'; batten for 'Devon Belle'
plate and rib along casing denoting asbestos 'Limpet' board composition. Photograph W. Hermiston, The Transport Treasury.**

21C3 ROYAL MAIL

Entered traffic 13 September 1941 to order No.1068.
Named on 24/10/41 at Waterloo station by Lord Essendon, Chairman of
Royal Mail lines. The engine was now in full malachite green livery.
*'...cabside windows are of wood and are painted green ...other alterations
...consist chiefly of the use of thinner plates ...reduction of weight of various
castings'.*
Renumbered 35003 May 1948
***For Tenders and Liveries - see separate
Sections.***

Allocations
Salisbury 9/41
Exmouth Jct. autumn 1942
To WR stock, 1/1/63
Nine Elms p/e 20/7/64
Bournemouth p/e 14/9/64
Weymouth p/e 17/10/66
Nine Elms p/e 17/4/67

Boilers
1092
1095 5/47
1094 3/55

Works: 2
(Mileages = since last General Overhaul)

14/5/53-16/5/53**NC**	*Axle examined for flaws only.*
22/6/53-8/8/53**HI**	
5/3/54-20/3/54**LC**	*205,486 miles. 'Test 2137, safety valve casings; Test 2242, coupling rods replaced'.*
10/2/55-19/3/55**GO**	*246,303 miles. 'Test 2242 twenty-two modifications, modified driving crank pin. Boiler pressure reduced, safety valves resited.*
6/12/55-14/1/56**LC-HC**	*44,963 miles. Two modifications.*
11/6/56-30/6/56**LC**	*65,626 miles.*
8/10/56-3/11/56**LI**	*87,484 miles. Four modifications.*
16/1/57-19/1/57**LC**	*102,309 miles. 'T2207 and left-hand side bogie spring renewed.*
8/1/58-1/2/58**LI**	*157,010 miles. One modification T2207. Drainpipe fitted to Tender TIA doser tank.*
7/11/58-29/11/58**LC**	*210,582 miles.*
11/6/59-29/8/59**GO**	*246,513 miles. Eleven modifications, three tests. BR type AWS fitted. Rebuilt having run 859,784 miles; tender tank rebuilt to 5,250 gallons*
22/11/60-17/1/61**LC**	*(Exmouth Junction shed)*
22/8/61-30/9/61**LI-HI**	*139,772 miles. Speedometer fitted and two tests.*
26/3/62-14/4/62**NC-LC**	*179,579 miles.*
4/4/63-25/5/63**LI-GO**	*228,110 miles. 'Tests 2296, 2305', spark arrester fitted.*
13/1/64-25/1/64**LC**	*34,813 miles. 'Tests 2296, 2305, 2326'.*
17/8/64-16/9/64**LC**	
19/5/65-2/7/65**I**	
5/1/67**NC**	

Works: 1

24/9/41	
23/11/41	
23/2/42	
18/5/42	
24/5/43	
9/44	*Smokebox hood fitted.*
11/8/45	*General Overhaul; new left-hand side cylinder fitted. 162,307 miles.*
17/3/47	
18/3/48	
15/6/48	
21/3/49	
20/3/50	*Cab modified.*
23/4/51	
18/2/52	

**Withdrawn July 1967 having run 1,131,793 miles. Stored at Nine Elms shed July to
October (approx.) 1967 and scrapped at J. Cashmore Ltd. Newport, South Wales in
December 1967.**

21C4 CUNARD WHITE STAR

Entered traffic 29 October 1941 to works order No.1068.
Named at Charing Cross station on 1/1/42 by Sir P.E. Bates, Chairman of Cunard White Star.
On loan to Nine Elms shed in place of 21C14, on 16 October 1946, 21C4 took a Pullman special from Waterloo-Southampton Docks for the first passenger sailing of 'Queen Elizabeth'. A trial run with ten Pullmans twelve days before had seen the first visit of the class to Southampton Docks.
Renumbered 35004 4/48.
For Tenders and Liveries - see separate Sections.

Allocations
Salisbury 10/41
Exmouth Jct. autumn 1942
Salisbury p/e 13/11/48.
Exmouth Jct. p/e 4/2/50
Salisbury p/e 1/4/57
Bournemouth p/e 14/9/64

Boilers
1093
1110 4/46
1123 10/50
1095 10/55

Works: 1	
23/2/42	
16/8/42	
23/9/42	
23/11/42	
26/7/43	
22/11/43	
7/44	
9/44	*Modified hood over smokebox.*
2/45	*New left-hand side cylinder.*
30/3/45	*General Overhaul. 124,306 miles.*
21/1/46	
22/4/46	
16/9/46	
20/1/47	
18/6/47	
14/2/48	
20/5/49	
21/8/50	*Modified cab fitted 10/50. Ex-works w/e 4/11/50; speedo fitted.*
22/1/51	
20/8/51	
17/3/52	
21/4/52	

Works: 2 *(Mileages = since last General Overhaul)*	
26/1/53-14/2/53**I**	
31/3/53-15/4/53**LC**	
12/5/53-14/5/53**NC**	*Axle examined for flaws only.*
27/7/53-7/8/53**NC**	
17/11/53-28/11/53**LC**	
2/6/54-26/6/54**LI**	*181,258 miles. Ten modifications; boiler pressure reduced.*
28/9/55-29/10/55**GO**	*248,081 miles. Twelve modifications, two tests; resited safety valves.*
7/3/56-24/3/56**LC**	*27,315 miles.*
7/3/57-30/3/57**LI-HI**	*89,845 miles. Two modifications, one test.*
27/8/57-31/8/57**NC**	*116,457 miles.*
21/2/58-26/2/58**NC**	*142,890 miles.*
16/5/58-5/7/58**GO**	*156,914 miles. Nine modifications. Rebuilt having run 750,886 miles.*
20/10/59-27/10/59**NC**	*92,761 miles. BR type AWS fitted.*
30/12/59-23/1/60**LI**	*104,647 miles. Three tests; speedometer fitted.*
11/5/60-19/5/60**NC**	*121,868 miles. 'T2319, 2321, 2322'.*
18/4/61-13/5/61**LI-HI**	*185,943 miles. One modification and three tests.*
23/8/62-15/9/62**NC-LC**	*254,407 miles.*
13/3/63-20/4/63**GO**	*272,537 miles. Spark arrester gear fitted.*
7/9/64-13/10/64**LC**	
26/8/65-1/10/65**LC**	

Withdrawn October 1965 having run 1,131,417 miles. Stored at Eastleigh Works from 9/65-1/66. Scrapped at Eastleigh shed (presumably it was unfit to move by rail?) by Cohen's in February 1966.
35004 had just been through the works, repaired and weighed, between 26 August and 14 October 1965 and had its mileage extended for a further 10,000 miles. It then had the mischance to slip severely near Hook while in charge of the 7.24am Bournemouth Central-Waterloo on 28 October and subsequently fail with broken and buckled coupling rods. Damage was relatively minor but such was the policy regarding steam stock that repairs were not authorised. It was this that spurred the creation of the Merchant Navy Locomotive Preservation Society (MNLPS) and eventually led to the purchase of 35028 from BR.

35004 CUNARD WHITE STAR in 'transition' state in early BR days, with original cab and still with its big gunmetal Southern roundel on the front but with sunshine BR number and lettering; at Exmouth Junction shed, off the down ACE. This was the engine shot at by a German raiding aircraft near Whimple in November 1942. Note the casing from the buffer beam to the rear of the cylinder; this got less and less as time went by! Photograph J.H. Aston.

35004 CUNARD WHITE STAR, light engine at Wilton; this would be 1948 or 1949, the second or third year of this Pullman train which changed engines out in the lonely Salisbury hinterland at Wilton (the first station to the west) and Exeter, maintaining the public timetable fiction that the train was non-stop to Sidmouth Junction. CUNARD WHITE STAR, then an Exmouth Junction engine, did the same job on the train's inaugural run the previous year. Photograph The Transport Treasury.

35004 CUNARD WHITE STAR spent most of its years based in the west, either at Exmouth Junction or Salisbury shed, only moving for the last year or so of its life, to Bournemouth. Sadly begrimed, it nevertheless rightly demands attention as it passes the shed yard at Salisbury on 18 April 1964, with the 1pm ex-Waterloo. Photograph Alec Swain, The Transport Treasury.

21C5 CANADIAN PACIFIC

Entered traffic 13 January 1942 to order No.1068.
Named at Victoria station 27/3/42 by Mr. F.W. Mottley of
Canadian Pacific.
*The front end of 21C5 had the front end of the casing altered to
reduce the difficulties caused by the exhaust beating down and
obscuring the driver's vision. The arrangement was generally
similar to that on 21C1 but differed in certain details.*
Renumbered 35005 4/48 (ran as s21C5 from March to April)
For Tenders and Liveries - see separate Sections.

Allocations
Salisbury 12/41
Exmouth Jct. autumn 1942
Nine Elms p/e 13/11/48
Exmouth Jct. p/e 12/5/51
Nine Elms p/e 19/3/54
Bournemouth p/e 26/11/59
Weymouth p/e 14/9/64

Boilers
1094
1091 1/48
1093 2/54

Works: 1
23/1/42	
4/44	Smokebox hood fitted.
26/8/44	
24/10/45	General Overhaul; new left-hand side cylinder fitted, 1/46. 158,606 miles.
18/11/46	
22/9/47	
15/12/47	
18/3/48	Fitting of mechanical stoker.
25/10/49-18/2/50	Heavy Intermediate; 57,886 miles run with stoker.
4/4/50	Mechanical stoker removed for comparative tests with hand firing.
31/5/50	Mechanical stoker refitted.
3/10/50	On 22/9/50 35005 failed on the 8.30am Waterloo-Weymouth near Woking and the train was worked forward by 31798. 35005 entered Eastleigh Works on 3/10/50 having been hauled in by 31875. It left the works on 18/11/50 having been fitted with a new right-hand side cylinder, rods and LMR self-cleaning smokebox equipment.
26/3/51	Mechanical stoker removed. 77,338 miles.
21/5/51	
24/9/51	

Works: 2
(Mileages = since last General Overhaul)
30/5/52-5/7/52**I**	
17/2/53-28/2/53**C**	
13/5/53-29/5/53**LC**	Done at Ashford Works; axle checked for flaws.
10/11/53-28/11/53**LC**	
1/1/54-13/2/54**GO**	165,589 miles. Valve chain adjustment, resited safety valves and modified steam reverser.
29/4/54-29/5/54**LC**	5,721 miles. New inside cylinder, boiler pressure reduced.
7/12/54-18/12/54**LC-HC**	38,335 miles. 'T2265'; new pattern coupling rods. Gauge wires fitted to coupling rod oil syphons at Eastleigh shed 14/2/55.
5/7/55-13/8/55**LI**	55,020 miles. Three modifications and three tests.
21/10/55-29/10/55	'Return' for previous LI, 63,871 miles. Three tests.
24/2/56-10/3/56**LC**	86,770 miles. One modification, three tests.
27/7/56-8/9/56**LI-HI**	106,857 miles. Right-hand cylinder replaced after cracks noted.
28/6/57-2/8/57**LC**	151,008 miles.
1/11/57-30/11/57**LI**	164,250 miles.
13/3/58-2/4/58**LC**	183,644 miles.
18/6/58-29/7/58**LC-HC**	196,167 miles.
2/4/59-30/5/59**GO**	227,317 miles. Ten modifications, four tests. Rebuilt having run 632,322 miles, tender tank rebodied.
14/11/60-3/12/60**LI**	98,641 miles. AWS and speedometer fitted.
9/4/62-12/5/62**LI**	190,736 miles.
26/2/63-16/3/63**LC**	240,012 miles.
28/11/63-1/2/64**LI-HI**	282,038 miles. Spark arrester fitted.

**Withdrawn 10/10/65 with tender 3348 after running 976,806 miles,
stored at Feltham 10/65-1/66 and Weymouth 1-3/66. Sold to Woodham
Brothers, Barry where it stayed 4/66-3/73. Spent a number of years at
Steamtown Carnforth before eventual restoration (with tender 3119,
ex-35009) on the Great Central Railway at Loughborough. After a short
period on the Mid-Hants Railway it is now based at Tyseley for main**

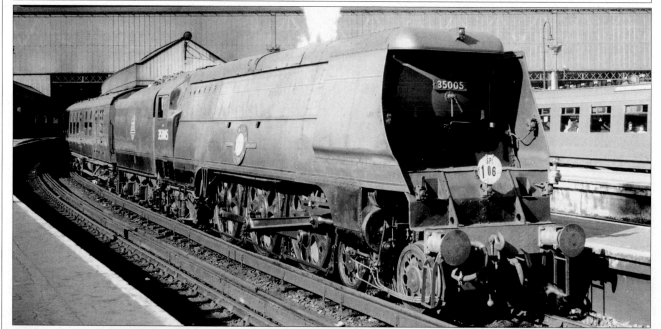

**35005 CANADIAN PACIFIC in green, at Waterloo in the mid-1950s, by which time the coupling rods were plain section. The
line of square marks climbing up the casing are the relics of the recording equipment attachments, put on during the
Rugby trials. Photograph T.R. Smith, The Transport Treasury.**

Late in the day and by now a Weymouth engine, but nevertheless resplendent for its WRS (Warwickshire Railway Society) special CANADIAN PACIFIC (there is a good view of the right-hand 'pocket') sits ready in the shed yard on 23 May 1965. New diesel shunters over to the right... Photograph Alec Swain, The Transport Treasury.

21C6 PENINSULAR & ORIENTAL S.N.Co.

Entered traffic 14 January 1942 to order No.1068.
Named at Ashford Works on 4/6/42 by Sir W. Currie, Chairman of the line.
When working an evening Exeter-Salisbury goods near Honiton on 17 December 1942 the chain parted in the oil bath on 21C6; the resulting fires had to be dealt with by the local fire brigade.
Renumbered 12/48 as 35006.

For Tenders and Liveries - see separate Sections.

Boilers
1095
1093 9/46
1111 12/48
1100 9/53
1119 7/55
1096 10/59

Allocation
At Salisbury all its working life.

Works: 2
(Mileages = since last General Overhaul)

12/8/52-12/9/52**I**	
12/5/53-14/5/53**NC**	*Examined for flaws in axles only.*
31/7/53-4/9/53**GO**	*Boiler pressure reduced.*
14/12/53-19/12/53**LC**	
2/6/54-4/6/54**NC**	*45,471 miles. Two modifications, 'T2195 and 2242'.*
	26/8/54 Weighing, one day, 62,242 miles.
13/1/55-12/2/55**LI**	*80,121 miles. Ten modifications, 'T2195 and 2242'.*
2/6/55-9/7/55**LC-HC**	*97,345 miles. Three modifications, 'T2195 and 2242', safety valves resited.*
19/4/56-5/5/56**LC-HC**	*134,790 miles.*
2/10/56-3/11/56**LI-HI**	*158,440 miles. Eight modifications, 'T2195 2207, 2242'.*
4/10/57-18/10/57**NC**	*213,374 miles. Modifications include: Steam chest pressure gauge pipe repositioned; cab handrails, left and right piston valve guide bushes, piston valve spindles and tail ends; platform clearance for reversing screw grease nipple.*
1/7/58-16/8/58**LI**	*253,172 miles. One modification, two tests.*
10/3/59-3/4/59**NC-LC**	*282,954 miles.*
5/8/59-10/10/59**GO**	*301,506 miles. Ten modifications, five tests, BR type AWS fitted. Rebuilt having run 962,757 miles.*
14/12/60-21/1/61**LI**	*84,308 miles. 'T2304 MN and WC inside big end cotters (new test)'. Speedometer fitted.*
11/4/62-5/5/62**NC-LC**	*178,728 miles.*
14/2/63-23/3/63**LI**	*216,496 miles.*

Works: 1

23/3/42	
22/10/42	
28/12/42	*Attention to chain drive gear.*
25/1/44	*General Overhaul; hood fitted over smokebox. 100,140 miles.*
July 1944	
18/12/44	
19/3/45	
24/10/45	
17/12/45	*New left-hand side cylinder fitted; 173,100 miles.*
15/7/46	
18/6/47	
13/9/48	
21/11/49	
22/1/51	*Modified cab fitted.*

Withdrawn in August 1964 after running 1,134,319 miles. Stored at Eastleigh shed 9/64-2/65 and moved to Woodham Brothers, Barry in 3/65. Left there in 3/83 for a new life on the Glos. & Warwickshire Railway, Toddington where it has been undergoing a comprehensive overhaul. It needed a new tender.

35006 PENINSULA & ORIENTAL S.N. Co., still with original cab and in malachite, alongside Exmouth Junction shed in 1950. As with almost anything where the Merchant Navys were concerned, the nameplate plaques had their own inconsistencies. Generally they were specifically left or right, fluttering in the wind towards the rear of the locomotive. Exceptions were 35006 and 35029 which had identical plates each side, so that the flag on one side (actually the right-hand) fluttered to the front. 35012 had right and left plates until 1951, when they were redesigned, the new ones being identical both sides. Photograph W. Hermiston, The Transport Treasury.

21C7 ABERDEEN COMMONWEALTH

Entered traffic June 1942 to order No.1068.
Named on 30/7/42 at Victoria station by Lord Essendon, Chairman of the Company.
Renumbered 35007 12/48.
For Tenders and Liveries - see separate Sections.

Boilers
1096
1108 7/47
1105 3/50
1118 6/55
1106 5/58

Allocations
Salisbury 6/42
Weymouth p/e 18/1/65
Nine Elms p/e 17/4/67

Works: 1

17/8/42	
23/11/42	
24/1/43	
24/6/43	New right-hand side cylinder.
24/4/44	Hood fitted over smokebox. General Overhaul 100,647 miles.
24/5/45	New left-hand side cylinder; 138,575 miles.
15/8/46	
16/12/46	
19/5/47	Inside cylinder replaced.
13/12/48	Inside cylinder replaced again.
3/50	Modified cab
21/5/51	

Works: 2
(Mileages = since last General Overhaul)

13/11/52-13/12/52**I**	
12/5/53-20/5/53**LC**	Driving axle examined for flaws.
24/11/53-24/12/53**HI**	
9/5/55-18/6/55**GO**	298,694 miles. Four modifications, 'T2268 and 2274', resited safety valves, boiler pressure reduced.
16/8/56-8/9/56**LI**	79,402 miles. Six modifications, two tests.
15/4/58-31/5/58**GO**	183,787 miles. Eight modifications, four tests. Rebuilt after running 799,299 miles.
9/9/59-26/9/59**LI**	92,117 miles. Outside cylinder barrel lubrication, BR type AWS fitted.
4/7/60-7/7/60**NC-LC**	143,038 miles.
7/3/61-8/4/61**LI-HI**	182,382 miles. 'T2305', speedometer fitted.
7/9/62-13/10/62**LI**	272,724 miles.
22/4/64-6/8/64**LI-HI**	
5/7/65-9/7/65**LC**	
11/8/66-23/9/66**LC**	

Withdrawn July 1967 having run 1,318,765 miles. Stored at Nine Elms shed 7/67-3/68 and scrapped at Buttigiegs, Newport, April 1968.

35007 ABERDEEN COMMONWEALTH on Honiton bank, 3 August 1955, in BR green and new cab. It was as 21C7 that the engine had some strange experimental smoke lifting measures applied in 1943. This involved a much wider gap under the 'widow's peak' and two rather flimsy, bolted-on deflector plates. Like the similar tinkerings with Gresley Pacifics, Royal Scots and so on, it was to no avail. Photographs W. Hermiston (see him standing by the hut in the picture below) and J. Robertson, The Transport Treasury.

21C8 ORIENT LINE

Entered traffic 16 June 1942 to order No.1068.
Named on 2/11/42 at Waterloo station by Mr. I.C. Geddes, Chairman of the Company.
Renumbered 35008 7/49.
For Tenders and Liveries - see separate Sections.

Boilers
1097
1092 8/47
1106 10/53
1102 5/57
1112 2/62

Allocations
Salisbury 6/42
Bournemouth p/e 8/2/54
Exmouth Jct. p/e 20/8/54
Bournemouth p/e 10/3/60
Weymouth p/e 17/10/66
Nine Elms p/e 17/4/67

Works: 1

22/10/42	
22/3/43	*Hood fitted over smokebox.*
26/7/43	
24/4/44	
14/9/44	*New left-hand side cylinder; General Overhaul 113,569 miles.*
20/8/45	
18/11/46	
18/6/47	*After collision with electric stock at Waterloo 10 June 1947, it was repaired still with a two window cab and boiler No.1092. Ex-works 30/8/47.*
19/4/49	*Fitted with three window cab. Ex-works 23/7/49.*
14/12/49	*New left-hand side cylinder.*
18/12/50	

Works: 2
(Mileages = since last General Overhaul)

22/4/52-17/5/52	**I**	
12/5/53-20/5/53	**LC**	*Driving axle examined for flaws.*
4/9/53-10/10/53	**GO**	*Safety valves resited.*
3/2/54-5/2/54	**NC**	*22,084 miles. 'T2081', regulator valve seating.*
19/8/54-4/9/54	**NC-LC**	*46,000 miles. 'Modification 176, T2081'; boiler pressure reduced.*
22/11/54-27/11/54	**LC**	*49,542 miles.*
14/2/55	**NC**	*Gauge wires fitted to coupling rod oil syphons at Eastleigh shed.*
14/4/55-7/5/55	**LI**	*70,677 miles. Six modifications, 'T2081 and 2242'.*
1/5/56-19/5/56	**LC**	*115,054 miles.*
15/10/56-10/11/56	**LI**	*140,392 miles. Five modifications, three tests.*
12/4/57-25/5/57	**GO**	*164,967 miles. Ten modifications, six tests. Rebuilt having run 730,712 miles.*
25/11/58-20/12/58	**LI**	*119,725 miles.*
23/3/60-23/4/60	**LI**	*209,216 miles. AWS and speedometer fitted.*
7/2/61-22/3/61	**LC**	*(Bricklayers Arms shop)*
24/11/61-3/2/62	**LI-GO**	*314,700 miles.*
W/E 3/2/62		*'Test 2305', driving coupling rod bushes.*
13/12/63-1/2/64	**LI-HI**	*94,542 miles. Spark arrester fitted.*
13/8/65-1/10/65	**LI**	

Withdrawn in July 1967 having run 1,286,418 miles. Stored at Nine Elms shed 7/67-3/68; scrapped at Buttigiegs, Newport in October 1968.

35008 ORIENT LINE out at work, a bit of a 'burn' on the lower part of the smokebox door. Photograph J.L. Stevenson, courtesy Hamish Stevenson.

35008 ORIENT LINE, up from Exeter for the day, on the ash road at Nine Elms. This picture is undated but the engine was rebuilt in May 1957; no pockets visible. It was the fitting side of things that derived the most benefit from the rebuilding of the Merchant Navys but though there was talk of valves and pistons going back to Eastleigh by the cartload before rebuilding it was never quite as bad as that. After rebuilding it is true that the sheds could deal with much more of the work, but this has to be balanced against the increased preparation time on the part of the driver – work, after all which Bulleid had sought to greatly reduce. Photograph W. Hermiston, The Transport Treasury.

21C9 SHAW SAVILL

Entered traffic 25 June, 1942 to order No.1068.
Named at Victoria station on 30/7/42 by Lord Essendon, Shaw Savill Chairman.
Renumbered 35009 8/49.
For Tenders and Liveries - see separate Sections.

Allocations
Salisbury 6/42
Exmouth Jct. p/e 1/4/57
WR 1/1/63

Boilers
1098
1097 11/47
1102 2/53
1117 3/57
1108 9/61

Works: 1
16/8/42
22/10/42
25/5/43   *Smokebox hood deflector.*
18/4/44   *General Overhaul, 103, 501 miles; ex-works 17/6/44.*
24/5/45
24/9/45   *New left-hand cylinder, 153,174 miles.*
17/10/46
22/9/47
21/2/49
20/6/49   *New inside cylinder.*
17/10/50
24/9/51
26/11/51
24/12/51   *New right-hand cylinder.*

Works: 2
(Mileages = since last General Overhaul)

20/1/53-27/2/53**GO**	*Cab modified.*
13/5/53-22/5/53**LC**	*Driving axle examined for flaws.*
30/12/53	*Weighing.*
5/5/54-12/6/54**LC**	*62,031 miles. Broken cylinder, modification No.81. Boiler pressure reduced.*
17/6/54-9/7/54	*'Return' for previous LC; 62,031 miles.*
19/8/54-11/9/54**LI**	*67,712 miles. Eleven modifications.*
23/12/55-28/1/56**LI**	*133,610 miles. Five modifications, 'T2268, 2274'.*
12/2/57-16/3/57**GO**	*182,356 miles. Six modifications, seven tests. Rebuilt having run 684,482 miles.*
15/8/58-13/9/58**LI**	*114,363 miles.*
22/1/60-13/2/60**LI**	*201,478 miles. 'T2304 inside big end cotters, speedometer fitted; T2310 eccentric strap bolts and locking plates; T2322 inside cylinder lubrication'.*
18/10/60-22/10/60**NC**	*245,301 miles. AWS fitted.*
25/7/61-16/9/61**GO**	*296,461 miles.*
20/11/61-6/1/62**NC-LC**	*9,562 miles*
7/11/62-15/12/62**LI-HI**	*76,329 miles.*
14/3/63-21/3/63**NC-LC**	

Withdrawn in September 1964 having run 1,127,542 miles with the same tender. Stored Exmouth Junction shed 10/64-2/65. Sold to Woodham Brothers, Barry where it stayed 3/65-2/89. After a number of years at Brighton is now being restored at Swindon; the plan is to base it on the Mid-Hants Railway.

The rebuilt SHAW SAVILL at Salisbury shed, where it spent the great part of its 'air-smoothed' days until transfer to Exmouth Junction.

21C10 BLUE STAR

Entered traffic 31 July 1942 to order No.1068.
Named 18/12/42 at Waterloo station by Lord Vestry, Chairman of the Company.
December 1942 saw it at Eastleigh Works in the unlikely role of mobile test bed, in the hope of curing the problems of drifting smoke. The outcome was an experimental hood fitted early in 1943 and, in the March, separate smoke deflectors.
Renumbered 35010 12/48.
For Tenders and Liveries - see separate Sections.

Boilers
1099
1090 1/48
1101 11/49
1124 5/51
1112 1/57
1105 11/61

Allocations
Salisbury 7/42
Nine Elms p/e 4/2/50
Bournemouth p/e 29/1/56
Exmouth Jct. p/e 10/3/60
Western Region stock 1/1/63
Bournemouth p/e 14/9/64

Works: 1
23/11/42
25/2/43
20/11/44   *General Overhaul,*
     120,033 miles; ex-works
     24/2/45.
24/10/45.
15/8/46
20/1/47   *New right-hand side*
     cylinder.
19/5/47
22/9/47
19/9/49   *Cab modified.*
26/3/51
21/5/51
18/6/51
17/3/52

Works: 2
(Mileages = since last General Overhaul)
16/10/52-15/11/52**I**
26/1/53-14/2/53**C**
9/4/53-15/4/53   *'Return' of previous Casual.*
13/5/43-16/5/53**NC**   *Done at Ashford Works, driving axle examined*
     for flaws.
20/4/54-15/5/54**LI**   *139,655 miles. Fourteen modifications, three tests, boiler pressure*
     reduced.
5/5/55-3/6/55**LI-HI**   *198,085 miles. Five modifications, four tests.*
21/11/56-5/1/57**GO**   *270,276 miles. Rebuilt having run 663,174 miles. Extensive*
     replacement of the main frames in front of the cylinders. Resited
     safety valves.
8/5/58-31/5/58**LI**   *95,448 miles.*
7/7/59-15/8/59**LI**   *181,810 miles. BR type AWS fitted.*
5/10/61-25/11/61**GO**   *337,822 miles. Speedometer fitted.*
W/E 2/12/61   *Briquette tube feeder fitted.*
21/3/62-7/4/62**NC-LC**   *17,371 miles.*
14/8/62-11/10/62**LC**   *(Exmouth Junction shed)*
12/3/63**LC**   *(Stewarts Lane shed)*
3/7/63-7/9/63**LI**   *96,341 miles. Spark arrester fitted.*
11/10/65-12/11/65**LC**
17/3/66-18/3/66**NC**

Withdrawn September, 1966, the main reason being a damaged right-hand cylinder. Mileage 1,241,299. Stored Eastleigh shed 9/66-3/67. Sold to Woodham Brothers, Barry where it stayed 4/67-1/85. First moved to North Woolwich it is now resident at Chappel & Wakes Colne, Essex, undergoing restoration.

21C10 BLUE STAR, climbing Honiton bank late in Southern days after its original wartime black gave way to malachite green. It got its BR number in '12/48', a year after nationalisation. Photograph J.L. Stevenson, courtesy Hamish Stevenson.

35010 BLUE STAR in almost preternaturally perfect external condition, in Eastleigh shed yard on 20 January 1957. This is more or less the locomotive's unveiling, its first day or so in steam in its new rebuilt guise. The tender, No.3120 which it had had from new, was modified at the same time. The trailing truck looks at first to have changed from the original cast unit to one of the later fabricated ones, but it turns out to be an original cast truck with a new cover over the top. The early crest appeared on the first ten rebuilds. Photograph Les Elsey.

21C11 GENERAL STEAM NAVIGATION

Entered traffic 30 December 1944 to order No.1189.
Named on 20/2/45 at Waterloo station by Mr. R. Kelso, Chairman of the Company.
Renumbered 35011 11/48.
For Tenders and Liveries - see separate Sections.

Boilers
1100
1111 1/47
1112 12/48
1104 9/50
1090 3/56
1097 7/59

Allocations
Nine Elms 12/44.
Bournemouth p/e 8/2/54
Nine Elms p/e 13/5/54
Exmouth Jct. p/e 12/6/57
Bournemouth p/e 10/3/60

Works: 1
19/3/45
24/9/45
17/10/46
13/9/48
22/8/49
20/7/50   *Modified Cab.*
24/9/51

Works: 2
(Mileages = since last General Overhaul)

17/4/53-16/5/53**LI**	
5/1/54-23/1/54**LC**	231,085 miles. Modification No.89, 'T2133' 3inch Ross safety valves. T2204; LMR steam heating relief valve.
14/5/54-5/6/54**LC**	239,460 miles. two modifications, boiler pressure reduced.
2/7/54-9/7/54**LC**	242,138 miles. Was a 'return' i.e. for readjustment to the work.
25/1/55-19/2/55**HI**	267,520 miles. Eleven modifications, three tests.
16/2/56-29/3/56**GO**	320,422 miles. Twelve modifications, two tests.
19/9/56-5/10/56**NC-LC**	31,394 miles.
19/6/57-3/8/57**LI**	68,076 miles. Four modifications, two tests.
9/10/58-25/10/58**LC**	154,086 miles.
5/12/58-13/12/58**LC**	159,051 miles.
7/5/59-4/7/59**GO**	180,942 miles. Eleven modifications, four tests. Rebuilt having run 670,782 miles.
20/4/61-20/5/61**LI-HI**	120,574 miles. AWS and speedometer fitted, long list.
17/10/62-1/12/62**LI**	218,584 miles.
13/6/63-29/6/63**NC-LC**	248,839 miles. Spark arrester fitted.
20/2/64-21/3/64**LC**	
2/2/65-19/3/65**LC**	

Withdrawn February, 1966 having run 1,069,128 miles. Stored at Eastleigh Works 2/66. Sold to Woodham Brothers, Barry and stayed there 3/67-3/89; moved to Brighton and now stored at Binbrooke Airfield, Lincolnshire. This loco, peculiarly, went for scrap with no middle crank axle…

21C11 GENERAL STEAM NAVIGATION, still with casing ahead of the cylinders and in its new malachite green livery, in either the 1947 or 1948 season – notice the peek-a-boo hole for the centre lamp under THE in the front board. (A bit of a mystery, for the Devon Belle rosters never involved running after dark!) 21C11 is the London engine (it was at Nine Elms for the first ten years from building) off the first leg Waterloo-Salisbury (Wilton) of the Devon Belle. 21C11 has turned and is ready to run back light to Wilton for the up train. Photograph J.L. Stevenson, courtesy Hamish Stevenson.

A very different 35011, rebuilt only in 1959. Here it is a few months later at Nine Elms, on 30 April 1960. Photograph J.L. Stevenson, courtesy Hamish Stevenson.

21C12 UNITED STATES LINE

Entered traffic 13 January 1945 to order No.1189.
Named at Waterloo station on 10/4/45 by Admiral Schuirman of the United States Navy.
Renumbered 35012 3/49
For Tenders and Liveries - see separate Sections.

Boilers
1102
1106 1/47
1104 3/49
1096 2/50
1101 7/52
1124 2/57
1120 4/62

Allocations
Nine Elms 1/45
Bournemouth p/e 8/2/54
Nine Elms p/e 13/5/54
Weymouth p/e 14/9/64
Nine Elms p/e 17/4/67

Works: 1
19/3/45	*Broken chain.*
20/1/47	
9/48	*Leading sandpipes blanked off.*
17/1/49	*Modified cab, ex-works w/e 19/3/49.*
14/12/49	
18/12/50	*Fitted with self-cleaning smokebox; ex-works w/e 17/2/51.*
20/8/51	*'Replica of company's house flag corrected'. Ex-works w/e 1/9/51.*
24/12/51	

Works: 2
(Mileages = since last General Overhaul)
6/5/52-5/7/52**GO**	*Boiler pressure reduced.*
4/6/53-12/6/53**LC**	*Driving axle replaced.*
20/11/53-19/12/53**HI**	
23/12/54-22/1/55**LI**	*138,262 miles. Two modifications, eight tests.*
20/1/56-18/2/56**LI**	*191,657 miles. Seven modifications, ten tests.*
25/1/57-28/2/57**GO**	*239,340 miles. Six modifications, nine tests. Rebuilt having run 564,821 miles.*
4/12/57-21/12/57**HC-LC**	*54,976 miles.*
2/12/58-24/12/58**LI**	*116,773 miles.*
27/10/59-7/11/59**NC**	*179,695 miles. BR type AWS fitted.*
19/12/59-18/1/60**LC**	*Done at Exmouth Junction.*
11/8/60-3/9/60**LI-HI**	*228,381 miles, speedo fitted.*
7/3/62-21/4/62**GO**	*315,907 miles.*
11/10/62-27/10/62**LC**	*26,238 miles.*
17/5/63-1/6/63**LC**	*57,349 miles.*
26/2/64-18/4/64**LI**	
29/7/64-19/8/64**LC**	
11/2/66-10/3/66**NC-LC**	

Withdrawn April 1967 after running 1,134,836 miles. Stored at Nine Elms shed 4-6/67 and at Weymouth shed 7/67-3/68. Sold to J. Cashmore, Newport and scrapped 4-9/68.
On 24 April 1964 A4 60008 DWIGHT.D.EISENHOWER, destined for the American Railroad Museum at Green Bay, was towed to Southampton docks by 35012, which in gleaming condition had also hauled all the dignitaries down from Waterloo. The museum's president made it known that upon withdrawal, they would very much welcome the addition of 35012, but the request fell on deaf ears and the loco was scrapped by Cashmore at Newport.

No Southern engines were particularly cosmopolitan and the Pacifics rarely wandered on to other Regions. With the 1960s, however, rail tours took Bulleid locos to some strange places indeed. These two fine side views of 35012 UNITED STATES LINES were taken as the engine turned at Kingmoor shed, of all places, on 13 June 1964. Photograph J.L. Stevenson, courtesy Hamish Stevenson.

21C13 BLUE FUNNEL at Bournemouth shed about 1947. Like 21C11 it spent the first decade of its life as a Nine Elms engine and was prominent on the revived 'Bournemouth Belle' of those years; the battens on the smoke deflectors indicate it was used on the Devon Belle too. Photograph J.L. Stevenson, courtesy Hamish Stevenson.

21C13 BLUE FUNNEL

Entered traffic 5 February 1945 to order No.1189.
Named at Waterloo station on 17/4/45 by Mr. L. Holt as BLUE FUNNEL LINE but these plates were soon removed; new plates read simply BLUE FUNNEL followed in Latin in smaller letters CERTUM PETE FINEM.
On 22 February 1945 worked the 8.30am down train from Waterloo station. On 19/1/ 47 took part in fifteen coach 500 ton test trains working between Norwood Junction and Brighton.
Renumbered 35013 7/48.
For Tenders and Liveries - see separate Sections.

Boilers
1104
1093 2/49
1112 12/52
1105 5/56
1119 5/61

Allocations
Nine Elms 2/45
Exmouth Jct. p/e 19/3/54
Western Region stock 1/1/63
Bournemouth p/e 14/9/64
Weymouth p/e 17/10/66
Nine Elms p/e 17/4/67

Works: 1
19/3/45
18/11/46
17/3/47
21/4/47 *Works visit due to boiler lagging fire.*
15/11/48
22/5/50
23/4/51

Works: 2
(Mileages = since last General Overhaul)

24/10/52-13/12/52**GO**	*Modified cab fitted.*
13/5/53-5/6/53**LC**	*Ashford Works, axle checked for flaws.*
16/2/54-27/3/54**LI**	*69,919 miles. Had to await cylinders, new inside one fitted.*
15/10/54-21/10/54**LC-NC**	*107,737 miles. Boiler pressure reduced.*
28/1/55-26/2/55**LI-HI**	*120,576 miles. Two modifications, eight tests.*
12/1/56-4/2/56**LC-HC**	*160,120 miles. Eight tests, one modification.*
6/4/56-19/5/56**GO**	*170,246 miles. Rebuilt having run 517,915 miles.*
20/7/56-26/7/56**NC-LC**	*10,012 miles.*
5/11/56-9/11/56**NC**	*28,173 miles. Five tests.*
7/1/57-11/1/57**LC**	*40,444 miles.*
18/6/57-29/6/57**LC**	*67,043 miles.*
6/3/58-29/3/58**LI**	*116,883 miles.*
3/3/59-9/4/59**LC**	*(Exmouth Junction shed)*
20/10/59-14/11/59**LI**	*237,881 miles. BR type AWS fitted.*
17/3/61-20/5/61**GO**	*325,057 miles. Speedometer fitted.*
8/3/62-17/3/62**NC**	*48,687 miles.*
22/10/62-8/11/62**LC**	*92,258 miles.*
30/1/64-21/3/64**LC-LI**	*'W/E 8/2/64, now holding, possible scrap'. Spark arrester fitted and three tests.*
29/12/65-25/2/66**LC**	

Withdrawn in July, 1967 having run 1,114,658 miles. Stored at Nine Elms shed 7-9/67 and scrapped at Buttigiegs, Newport, 10/67.
By January 1967 many of the SR engineering works and speed restrictions had been lifted, and crews took the opportunity to 'have a last fling' with steam. On 28 April 35013 left Waterloo fourteen minutes late with twelve coaches and a van, and reached Winchester *one minute early*. The speed recorder was firmly jammed at 104mph. More was to come and on 26 June 1967 35013 attained 106mph!

BLUE FUNNEL at Waterloo – note AWS, pockets, new BR tender emblem. It had emerged rebuilt in May 1956 and bore the name BLUE FUNNEL CERTUM PETE FINEM. It had got plates bearing just BLUE FUNNEL LINE in April 1945 but because they were presumably incorrect in some way, were soon after replaced by new plates with the Latin phrase added. A simple BLUE FUNNEL was its customary sobriquet, however. Photograph The Transport Treasury.

21C14 NEDERLAND LINE

Entered traffic 13 February 1945 to order No.1189.
Named at Waterloo station on 27/11/45 by Mr. A.F. Bronsing, Managing Director of the line.
Week ending 28/9/46 used on coal tests between Exeter and Salisbury, sixteen coaches and twelve the following week. On 1/10/46 it covered the 88 miles Exeter-Salisbury in 86 minutes on the 10.25am Exeter Central to Waterloo. Return working was the 2.43pm Salisbury-Exeter. Replaced by 21C4 (on loan) at Nine Elms shed.
Renumbered 35014 5/49.
For Tenders and Liveries - see separate Sections.

Allocations
Nine Elms 2/45
Exmouth Jct. p/e 13/5/54
Bournemouth p/e 10/8/54
Stewarts Lane p/e 4/6/55
Nine Elms p/e 5/6/56
Weymouth p/e 14/9/64

Boilers
1106
1100 2/47
1106 5/49
1107 8/51 (minus thermic syphons)
1103 10/53
1123 7/56
1116 3/62

Works: 1

19/3/45	*New inside cylinder.*
20/8/45	
18/11/46	
9/47	*Cab and firebox sheeting damaged; repaired Nine Elms.*
18/3/48	
21/2/49	*Modified cab fitted.*
18/4/50	*Test 2162; 'bronze bushes, Anti-Attrition Co.'*
18/6/51	
19/5/52	

Works: 2
(Mileages = since last General Overhaul)

22/5/52-24/5/52**NC**	
14/10/52-8/11/52**I**	
24/2/53-27/2/53**C**	
12/5/53-26/5/53**LC**	*Ashford Works; axle checked for flaws.*
1/10/53-7/11/53**GO**	
17/6/54-3/7/54**LC**	*30,828 miles. 'Modifications 81 and 176, T2204'. Boiler pressure reduced, safety valves resited.*
11/3/55-9/4/55**LI**	*71,156 miles. Four modifications, standard valve renewal.*
2/3/56-30/3/56**LC**	*(Bricklayers Arms shop)*
18/5/56-7/7/56**GO**	*108,460 miles. Tender 3126 fitted 7/7/56. Rebuilt having run 516,811 miles.*
6/6/57-15/6/57**LC**	*68,976 miles. Six tests.*
2/6/58-28/6/58**LI**	*136,675 miles.*
22/9/59-17/10/59**LI**	*236,082 miles. BR type AWS fitted.*
11/11/60-3/12/60**LC-HI**	*308,354 miles. AWS overhauled and speedometer fitted.*
1/6/61-1/7/61**LC**	*335,897 miles. New right-hand cylinder.*
31/1/62-17/3/62**GO**	*375,945 miles.*
4/9/63-26/10/63**LI-HI**	*88,686 miles.*
2/7/65	*'No work carried out'.*
17/3/66-12/4/66**LC**	
25/5/56-8/6/66**NC**	

Withdrawn in March, 1967 having run 1,062,394 miles. Stored at Weymouth shed, 6-8/67. Scrapped at J. Cashmore, Newport, 9/67.

35014 NEDERLAND LINE prepared for the Devon Belle about 1950 – note cover on slidebar and sanding still on all three coupled wheels. 35014 was yet another Nine Elms engine at the time; there is no description on the photograph but it is certainly not the London end of operations; instead, this is the very end of Salisbury shed yard (look at the ash-buried state of the track in the foreground) with the engine pointing down towards Wilton where the engines changed. This would

21C15 ROTTERDAM LLOYD

Entered traffic 5 March 1945 to order No.1189.
Named at Waterloo station on 27/11/45 by Mr W. Ruys, Managing Director of the Company.
Worked the inaugural Devon Belle on 20/6/47 to and from Wilton.
Renumbered 35015 6/49.
For Tenders and Liveries - see separate Sections.

Allocations
Nine Elms 3/45
Stewarts Lane p/e 5/6/56
Nine Elms p/e 14/6/59
'Stored unserviceable 6/1/64'

Boilers
1105
1107 2/47
1121 6/49
1099 4/54
1113 6/58
1091 6/62

Works: 1
20/8/45
18/11/46
16/12/46
22/9/47   *New right-hand cylinder.*
20/11/47
21/3/49   *Modified cab and new inside cylinder.*
18/4/50   *Second new right-hand cylinder.*
18/12/50
17/3/52

Works: 2
(Mileages = since last General Overhaul)

7/5/53-6/6/53**HI**	
9/11/53-28/11/53**LC**	
23/3/54-24/4/54**GO**	*229,860 miles. Fifteen modifications, boiler pressure reduced, resited safety valves, etc.*
1/6/54-12/6/54**NC**	*2,754 miles. Three tests, oil pump examined and replaced.*
8/12/55-23/12/55**LC**	*(Bricklayers Arms shop)*
29/5/56-30/6/56**LI-HI**	*81,033 miles. Coal weighing tender 3343 attached on 7/7/56, two tests; eight modifications.*
19/6/57-6/7/57**LC**	*115,587 miles. 'T2265 and 2268': left-hand cylinder from 35016.*
1/5/58-14/6/58**GO**	*133,392 miles. Tender 3123 attached, ten modifications, three tests, new left-hand cylinder. Rebuilt having run 549,706 miles.*
27/10/59-7/11/59**NC**	*49,027 miles. BR type AWS fitted.*
2/1/60-29/1/60**LC**	*(Nine Elms shed)*
25/5/60-18/6/60**LI-HI**	*81,987 miles. Speedometer fitted.*
5/10/61-16/12/61**LC**	*(Bricklayers Arms shop)*
14/5/62-16/6/62**HC**	*188,485 miles.*
28/12/62-9/1/63**LC**	*211,890 miles.*

Withdrawn February 1964 having run 813,950 miles. Stored at Nine Elms shed 1-7/64 and scrapped at Slag Reduction Co. Rotherham, 12/64.

make it the engine off the down leg, going back to shed for turning and then off again light to Wilton. (Strictly speaking, whether it went back to Wilton depended on the day of the week. In 1950 the Devon Belle ran down only on Thursdays, both ways Friday, Saturday, Sunday and Monday and up only on Tuesdays.) No legend on tender – no malachite green Merchant Navy ever did get the BR crest. Photograph W. Hermiston, The Transport Treasury.

21C16 ELDERS FYFFES

Entered traffic 14 March 1945 to order No.1189.
Named on 5/7/45 at Waterloo station by Mr H. Stockley, managing director of the Company.
On 23 March 1945 it worked the 9.54am Waterloo to Basingstoke – '...this seems to be the regular test run for these locomotives.'
Renumbered 35016 10/48
For Tenders and Liveries - see separate Sections.

Boilers
1107
1112 1/47
1094 10/48
1111 8/54
1110 4/57
1124 8/62

Allocations
Nine Elms 3/45
Weymouth p/e 14/9/64

Works: 1
24/5/45	*Attention to middle cylinder and oil bath.*
18/11/46	*All cylinders rebored.*
16/8/48	
18/10/48	
20/5/49	*Cab modified.*
20/3/50	
22/5/50	
20/8/51	

Works: 2
(Mileages = since last General Overhaul)

16/2/53-14/3/53**LI**	
30/6/53-10/7/53**NC**	
18/1/54-30/1/54**LC**	245,586 miles. 'Modification No.89'.
6/7/54-27/8/54**GO**	274,356 miles. Twelve modifications, boiler pressure reduced and safety valves resited.
23/11/55-31/12/55**LI**	61,695 miles. Awaited new axle boxes – on 16/11/55 fractures occurred on all four coupling rods and cracks appeared in axleboxes near Gillingham, Dorset. The result was a redesign of the coupling rods and steel axleboxes on the rebuilds.
28/8/56-15/9/56**NC-LC**	102,074 miles. Valve and piston exam.
13/3/57-17/4/57**GO**	117,667 miles. Eight modifications, five tests. Rebuilt having run 467,091 miles, including new left-hand cylinder.
25/9/58-18/10/59**LI**	101,610 miles.
15/10/59-7/11/59**LI**	170,265 miles. BR type AWS fitted.
31/1/61-25/3/61**LI-HI**	251,080 miles. Speedometer fitted.
21/6/62-18/8/62**GO**	323,115 miles.
26/9/62-29/9/62**NC**	
30/5/63-31/7/63**LC**	*(Bricklayers Arms shop)*
2/3/64-4/4/64**LC**	
25/11/64-18/12/64**NC-LC**	

Withdrawn 8 August 1965 having run 900,637 miles. Stored at Weymouth shed 8-11/65 and scrapped at Birds, Bridgend, Glamorgan in 12/65.

Above. A striking, beautiful blue 35016 ELDERS FYFFES at Eastleigh in the mid-1950s, alongside the vast water tank building (still with wartime whitewash); sanding abandoned on front wheel though top sliding hatch still looks usable. Photograph W. Hermiston, The Transport Treasury.

Top left. 35015 ROTTERDAM LLOYD, just ex-works and newly renumbered in June 1949, at Eastleigh. Another engine which spent its first ten years at Nine Elms; covered slidebars, Devon Belle batten, no legend on tender and black front skirt. It later ran with the coal weighing tender. Sufficient superlatives, it must be said, hardly exist to do justice to the exquisite condition of many of the originals in these years. This was the last time a Merchant Navy was repainted in malachite green – a quite beautiful sight. (As a matter of interest, all of the 21C11-21C20 batch went new to Nine Elms and stayed there for years.) Photograph W. Hermiston, The Transport Treasury.

Bottom left. ROTTERDAM LLOYD went to the Eastern Section from 1956 to 1959, the only time it spent away from Nine Elms, though it was only based a five minute walk away at Stewarts Lane. While down the road with the 'Battersea lot' it was rebuilt in 1958; here it is, made ready at Stewarts Lane for 'the Arrer' on 21 March 1959. Photograph R.C. Riley.

ELDERS FYFFES reconstructed, in that classic location, the bombed site of the 'Old Shed' at Nine Elms, 22 August 1958. The work of remodelling was directed by R.G. Jarvis at Brighton, working under H.H. Swift, who had succeeded Bulleid. The original outside cylinders were retained and only the inside cylinder replaced, though where outside cylinders were in poor condition they were replaced by new ones cast off the old pattern. Photograph W. Hermiston, The Transport Treasury.

The perfect portrait or, dare it – *Rhapsody in Blue*? Immaculate and striking, 35017 BELGIAN MARINE stands on the coaling road at Nine Elms in blue, 16 July 1949, on the occasion of a visitation from Maurice Earley's Railway Photographic Society. Photograph E.D. Bruton.

21C17 BELGIAN MARINE

Entered traffic 17 April 1945 to order No.1189.
Named at Victoria station 22/10/45 by Monsieur G. Rongvaux,
then Belgian Minister of Communications.
Renumbered 35017 4/48.
For Tenders and Liveries - see separate Sections.

Boilers
1108
1101 5/47
1122 7/49
1114 7/54
1107 3/57
1109 9/63

Allocations
Nine Elms 4/45
Weymouth p/e 14/9/64

Works: 1

24/9/45	
21/4/47	
14/2/48	*Prepared for the Locomotive Exchanges, fitted with Flaman speed recorder, modified cab; LMS tender 10123 fitted w/e 24/4/48. Worked Kings Cross-Leeds and Euston-Carlisle.*
20/5/48	
19/4/49	
21/7/49	
22/5/50	*New left-hand cylinder.*
17/10/50	
23/7/51	

Works: 2
(Mileages = since last General Overhaul)

5/3/53-28/3/53	**LI**	
13/5/53-6/6/53	**LC**	*Done at Ashford Works, axles checked for flaws.*
15/6/54-31/7/54	**GO**	*278,616 miles. Thirteen modifications, boiler pressure reduced, safety valves resited.*
14/11/55-10/12/55	**LI-HI**	*72,587 miles. Seven modifications, three tests.*
26/2/57-30/3/57	**GO**	*135,397 miles. Seven modifications, six tests. Rebuilt having run 594,522 miles.*
20/5/58-21/6/58	**LC-HI**	*80,758 miles. Two modifications, three tests.*
28/9/59-24/10/59	**LI**	*163,007 miles. Outside cylinder barrel lubrication, BR type AWS fitted.*
22/2/61-1/4/61	**LI**	*243,723 miles. Speedometer fitted.*
13/4/62-5/5/62	**LC**	*297,132 miles.*
5/7/63-21/9/63	**GO**	*333,177 miles. Spark arrester fitted.*
30/3/65-14/5/65	**LI**	

Withdrawn in July 1966 having run 1,017,754 miles. Stored at Weymouth shed 7-8/66 and scrapped (with tender 3114) at Buttigiegs, Newport in September 1966.

35017 BELGIAN MARINE, rebuilt in the early part of 1957, outside the 'New Shed' at Nine Elms, 6 September 1958. That is the ashpan operating handle being handed down from the footplate. The general idea was to keep what was regarded as good, which was a very large part of the design, and jettison only what was 'bad'. Rebuilding thus kept the great glory at the heart of the original design, the tremendous steam producing capacity of its boiler. Whatever the advantages of the rebuilds so far as maintenance and repair were concerned, everything had a price and the benefits of the transition should not be wildly overstated; daily preparation time increased of course and the need to fit 'stink bomb' detectors (they released an intense aniseed smell when overheated) to the inside big ends speaks for itself. Out on the road, too, the advantages were less clear cut than has often been claimed; the new screw reverser could physically test the older and stouter driver and certainly the new locos were less free running and smooth riding than the originals, while not all firemen approved of the power-operated firehole doors being removed. Photograph R.C. Riley.

Engines could hardly appear in a cleaner condition than this; it is almost unreal (it had been specially prepared for BR official photographs) and is beautifully captured by the photographer in the clear winter light. 35018 BRITISH INDIA LINE stands blinking in the sunlight in the works yard, 7 February 1956. Note how the feed pipes to the clack valves take that sudden change of direction and the curiously high front sand filler, different from the other rebuilds. The first to be rebuilt, BRITISH INDIA LINE was slightly different from the production run and always easy to spot for these reasons. This was true from the other side too, where the bend in the ejector pipe came above the left-hand nameplate. On all the others the bend occurred just to the rear of the smokebox. Note – deflector handrails have not yet been fitted. Photograph Les Elsey.

35019 FRENCH LINE C.G.T., just rebuilt and ex-works, 23 May 1959. The first part of the name, oddly, was in a joined-up 'ooh la la' jaunty script; this was unexpected but, it turns out, the Southern was merely reproducing the shipping company's own style. Its second series 5,100 gallon tender was done at the same time, emerging with the later BR emblem from the first. The fitting staff at sheds – the men with unfeasibly large spanners you might say – were not so much concerned with the time taken for the work so far as the original engines were concerned. After all they got paid for the day's work and had not all designers ('them') been imbeciles in the way they arranged their creations since time began? What fitting staff heartily *loathed* was getting overalls *soaked* in oil; it went through to the clothes underneath and the stink followed you back to the cabin afterwards. The rebuilds ended this. Photograph Peter Groom.

More of the Devon Belle – 35020 BIBBY LINE, here in blue and the engine notable for the huge smoke deflectors. At Nine Elms for almost all its life, it is standing in Salisbury shed yard ready to run back to Wilton and collect the up working of the observation car Pullman train. The Flaman speed recorder, the bracket for which survives, was fitted when the engine was made 'spare' for the 1948 Locomotive Exchanges. Date (note slidebar cover) is about 1950. Photograph W. Hermiston, The Transport Treasury.

21C18 BRITISH INDIA LINE

Entered traffic 7 May 1945 to order No.1189.
Named at Waterloo station 13/12/45 by Mr. A.J. Lang, Managing Director of the British India Steam Navigation Co. Ltd.
When new the driving wheels were fabricated and in 4/47 were replaced by standard cast type; worked the first post-war Bournemouth Belle on 7/10/46.
Renumbered 35018 in 5/48.
For Tenders and Liveries - see separate Sections.

Boilers
1109
1105 4/47
1100 9/49
1109 7/51
1116 1/56
1117 12/61

Allocations
Nine Elms 5/45
Bournemouth p/e 24/11/60
Nine Elms p/e 17/1/61

Works: 1
23/7/45
24/10/45
21/5/46
17/3/47 *Fabricated driving wheels replaced by standard cast type.*
21/4/48 *Flaman speed recorder fitted, cab modified for the Locomotive Exchanges which 35018 worked Waterloo-Exeter.*
19/4/49
21/7/49
22/6/50 *New right-hand cylinder.*
21/5/51
22/10/51

Works: 2
(Mileages = since last General Overhaul)
10/6/52-4/7/52**LC**
7/7/52-11/7/52**NC**
29/9/52-14/10/52**NC**
8/4/53-2/5/53**LI**
4/6/53-12/6/53**LC** *Driving axle replaced.*
2/12/53-16/12/53**LC**
28/6/54-7/8/54**LI-HI** *163,214 miles. Fourteen modifications, boiler pressure reduced.*
16/11/55-14/2/56**GO** *First of class to be rebuilt, having run 504,900 miles.*
16/4/56-17/4/56**NC** *5,478 miles.*
25/9/56-4/10/56 *Valve & piston exam. Brighton Works.*
8/3/57-13/3/57**LC** *65,288 miles. Five tests.*
14/5/58-14/6/58**LI** *141,359 miles. Five tests.*
24/4/59-8/5/59**NC** *208,857 miles.*
14/1/60-6/2/60**LI** *230,295 miles. Speedometer fitted, four tests.*
2/12/60-10/12/60**NC** *299,519 miles. AWS fitted, three tests.*
7/11/61-13/1/62**GO** *329,263 miles. Tender 3118 fitted.*
10/4/62-19/4/62**NC** *3,894 miles. Four tests.*
17/5/63-12/7/63**LC** *At Bricklayers Arms shed.*
23/8/63-7/9/63**LC** *82,681 miles. Four tests.*

Withdrawn in August, 1964 having run 956,544 miles. Stored at Nine Elms shed 8/64-2/65. Sold to Woodham Brothers, Barry and stored there, with tender 3343 3/65-3/80. Sold to the Mid-Hants Railway with tender 3350 and undergoing long term restoration. (Tank from 3350 later sold to the 35025 Brocklebank Line Association.)

21C19 FRENCH LINE C.G.T.

Entered traffic 7 June 1945 to order No.1189.
Named at Southampton Docks 22/9/45 by Monsieur de Malglaive, director of the line.
Took part in the 1948 Locomotive Exchanges 4/48 fitted with a modified cab, a Flaman speed recorder and LMS tender 10219. It worked Kings Cross-Leeds for two days before suffering firebox defects and after attention worked Paddington-Plymouth
Renumbered 35019 4/48 (Was s21C19 in Eastleigh Works in March, but emerged fully renumbered.)
For Tenders and Liveries - see separate Sections.

Allocations
Nine Elms 6/45
Weymouth p/e 4/9/64

Boilers
1103
1102 1/50
1108 6/51
1100 10/55
1092 5/59

Works: 1
20/8/45
21/3/46
18/6/47
18/8/47 *Cylinders rebored due to excessive wear*
14/2/48 *Cab fitted (as 35019) to suit LMS tender No.10219 w/e 17/4/48*
20/5/48
21/3/49
20/10/49
23/4/51 *Single nozzle blastpipe and chimney fitted; ex-works 23/6/51.*
23/7/51 *'Arrived for further adjustment.'*
24/12/51 *Chimney alteration included a flared skirt to the petticoat 'with its single exhaust, when working hard, it gave a very creditable imitation of a Paddlebox in full cry'*

Works: 2
(Mileages = since last General Overhaul)
13/3/53-6/6/53**HI**
3/12/53-24/12/53**LC**
18/2/54-27/2/54**LC** *114,787 miles. Steam heating relief valve repositioned; single blast pipe and small diameter chimney.*
9/8/54-4/9/54**LI-HI** *139,752 miles. Boiler pressure reduced. Fifteen modifications*
13/4/55-30/4/55**LC-HC** *175,633 miles. Modern crank axle sprocket, wheel and deflector plate fitted to diagram W11228.*
26/7/55-14/10/55**LC-GO** *182,950 miles. Converted to General Overhaul after boiler failure, seven modifications. Resited safety valves.*
1/3/56-17/3/56**LC** *31,525 miles. Chimney and blastpipe converted to standard.*
7/9/56-6/10/56**LI** *61,438 miles. Three modifications, two tests.*
11/9/57-5/10/57**LI** *109,465 miles. Two modifications, three tests.*
24/10/58-8/11/58**LC** *158,087 miles.*
17/3/59-15/5/59**GO** *164,868 miles. Ten modifications, two tests. Rebuilt having run 617,368 miles plus three new cylinders.*
9/10/59-16/10/59**NC** *30,824 miles. BR type AWS fitted.*
11/3/60-26/3/60**LI-NC** *52,407 miles. Inside big end heat detector modified.*
12/1/61-11/2/61**LI-HI** *106,608 miles. Speedometer fitted.*
15/3/62-24/3/62**NC** *175,506 miles. Three tests*
11/2/63-16/3/63**LI** *220,458 miles. Three tests*
27/5/64-26/6/64**NC-LC**

Withdrawn 5 September 1965 having run 947,344 miles. Stored at Weymouth shed 9-12/65 and at Salisbury shed 1/66. Scrapped at J.Cashmore, Newport in January, 1966.

35020 BIBBY LINE, pristine with 6,000 gallon tender, in the shed yard at Eastleigh on 20 May 1961. Note shorter necks to the sand fillers – the longer necks in the rebuilds also made for sand spillage, and some, at least, were changed in their turn. When BIBBY LINE was rebuilt in 1956 it was chosen for testing at Swindon and on the road, to compare a rebuilt engine with the original that had been so exhaustively examined back in 1953, 35022 HOLLAND-AMERICA LINE. The results were happy in the extreme, with almost perfect combustion and an increase in cylinder efficiency of something like a fifth. Photograph Les Elsey.

Left. 35021 NEW ZEALAND LINE brand new, 11 September 1948, in beautiful shiny (partly varnished) malachite green. Delays in building the tenders at Brighton meant NEW ZEALAND LINE had to go into traffic with this light Pacific tender. The name stayed covered up until November when a proper 6,000 gallon one was available and the naming ceremony could proceed after finish painting and lining. Photograph H.C. Casserley.

Left. NEW ZEALAND LINE at Nine Elms, 17 August 1956, with its correct third series 6,000 gallon tender. BR green with rectangular panels on the cab and modified tender. Front sand filler resolutely blocked off and hardly any trace left. Photograph J. Robertson, The Transport Treasury.

21C20 BIBBY LINE

Entered traffic 30 June 1945 to order No.1189.
Named at Waterloo station 18/10/45 by Mr H. Bibby, Chairman of the Company.
*Prepared for the Locomotive Exchanges by having a modified cab, a Flaman
speed recorder extra long smoke deflectors amd LMS tender (No.10373) but
did not take part.*
Renumbered 35020 5/48.
For Tenders and Liveries - see separate Sections.

Allocations
Nine Elms 7/45
Weymouth p/e 14/9/64

Boilers	
1102	
1109	7/47
1103	5/50
1096	6/53
1108	4/56
1100	4/61

Works: 1

24/5/45	
23/7/45	
24/9/45	
21/4/47	
18/3/48	*Extra long smoke deflectors.*
20/5/48	
20/6/49	
22/2/50	*TIA water treatment equipment fitted and new inside cylinder; Flaman speed recorder removed.*
23/4/51	

Works: 2
(Mileages = since last General Overhaul)

19/5/52-21/6/52**LI**	
1/5/53-2/7/53**GO**	*Safety valves resited. Admitted to works after driving axle fractured on 24/4/53 at speed near Crewkerne.*
18/5/54-21/5/54**NC**	*66,076 miles. 'Modification No.176', boiler pressure reduced.*
5/11/54-27/11/54**LI-HI**	*83,025 miles. Seven modifications and tests.*
25/7/55-20/8/55**LC-HC**	*118,734 miles. Two modifications, six tests, new inside cylinder.*
15/3/56-28/4/56**GO**	*153,451 miles. Rebuilt having run 507,958 miles. Tender 3345 attached 2/6/56 for tests on Swindon Plant; 3344 attached 7/7/56.*
20/5/57-1/6/57**LC**	*60,018 miles.*
11/2/58-8/3/58**LI**	*113,007 miles. Modified whistle valve springs.*
4/5/59-15/5/59**LC**	*191,469 miles.*
26/6/59-1/8/59**LI**	*195,017 miles. BR type AWS fitted.*
2/3/61-29/4/61**GO**	*289,003 miles. Speedometer fitted.*
18/2/63-23/3/63**LI-HI**	*91,750 miles.*

Withdrawn February 1965 having run 981,479 miles. Stored and cut up at Eastleigh Works 3/65. Only one of the class to be scrapped at its place of birth. (Record Card says 'Scrap at Eastleigh 20.2.65')

35021 NEW ZEALAND LINE starts with the 1.30pm ex-Waterloo after a signal stop at Basingstoke, 4 August 1964. AWS fitted by now, though the Southern was something of a laggard when it came to this system – all that third rail around could make for some extraordinary 'magnetic field interference' problems. Some Merchant Navys had still not been equipped even by 1962, and some, though the record card records the fixing of AWS never got it, whatever the cards say. Photograph Alec Swain, The Transport Treasury.

35021 NEW ZEALAND LINE

Entered traffic 11 September 1948 to order No.3393.
Named at Waterloo station on 24/11/48 by Mr. H.S. Whitehouse, Chairman of the Company.
Boiler 1098 had been carried by 21C9 from 6/42-11/47 and the firebox was renewed. This third series of the class had wedge shaped cabs, three side windows and fabricated rear truck. Ashford built the frames and cylinders, Brighton the boilers and tenders (all with TIA water treatment) while Eastleigh constructed the remainder of the parts and undertook assembly of all the 'third batch'.
For Tenders and Liveries - see separate Sections.

Boilers
1098 (first fitted to 21C9)
1091 10/54
1098 6/59

Allocations
Exmouth Jct. 9/48
Nine Elms p/e 12/5/51
Bournemouth p/e 12/6/57

Works: 1
21/11/49
20/9/50
21/1/52   *Ex-works w/e 1/3/52 with modified tender.*

Works: 2
(Mileages = since last General Overhaul)
5/5/52-10/5/52**NC**
8/7/53-22/8/53**HI**
4/2/54-19/2/54**LC**   *293,512 miles. Modification 'No.169', modified crank pin and plate. 'T2231' tender raves and tool pockets.*
22/5/54-11/6/54**LC**   *306,066 miles. Modification 'No.81, T2231'.*
26/8/54-8/10/54**GO**   *314,960 miles. Thirteen modifications, 'T2231'. Boiler pressure reduced and safety valves resited.*
23/9/55-8/10/55**LC**   *62,020 miles. Two modifications, 'T2231'.*
13/1/56-17/2/56**LI**   *80,104 miles. Seven modifications, two tests.*
17/1/57-9/2/57**LI**   *135,516 miles. Two modifications, three tests.*
30/8/57-14/9/57**LC**   *177,700 miles.*
25/3/58-25/4/58**LI-HI**   *203,188 miles. Three modifications, 'T2285'.*
23/4/59-13/6/59**GO**   *260,033 miles. Ten modifications, three tests. Rebuilt having travelled 575,993 miles.*
24/3/61-22/4/61**LI**   *13,468 miles. AWS gear and speedometer fitted.*
2/11/62-8/12/62**LI**   *209,472 miles.*
14/2/64-21/3/64**LC**

Withdrawn 8 August 1965 having run 859,661 miles. Stored at Eastleigh Works 9/65 and scrapped with tender 3126 at Birds, Bridgend, Glamorgan, 10/65.

The rebuilt 35022 HOLLAND AMERICA LINE at the Salisbury coal stage late on; about 1962 probably, given the AWS battery box on the buffer beam and the still-SR shed code. That smokebox, retaining the original door and forming such a strong and prominent feature of the rebuilt engines was central to the design. It was properly circular for a start, resting on a saddle which was formed partly of a new fabricated saddle stretcher and partly of the new steel inside cylinder casting below. This gave much greater strength to the framing at the front end. Photograph B. Richardson, The Transport Treasury.

35022 HOLLAND-AMERICA LINE

Entered traffic 9 October 1948 to order No.3393.
Named at Southampton Docks on 24/1/49 by Mr W.H. de Monchy,
Managing Director of the shipping line.
For Tenders and Liveries - see separate Sections

Boilers
1099 (first fitted to 21C10, now with new firebox)
1107 11/53
1109 6/56
1123 7/62

Allocations
Exmouth Jct. 10/48
Bournemouth p/e 22/6/54
Exmouth Jct. p/e 10/3/60
Western Region stock 1/1/63
Nine Elms p/e 2/3/64
Weymouth p/e 14/9/64

Works: 1
13/12/48
15/5/50-5/7/50**HI** 92,805 miles
10/12/51-8/2/52**LI** 188,928 miles

Works: 2
(Mileages = since last General Overhaul)

2-5/53	*Single nozzle blastpipe fitted.*
18/5/53-28/5/53**LC**	*Single blastpipe – Rugby Trials.*
22/7/53-8/8/53**LC**	
22/10/53-21/11/53**HC**	
19/12/54	*Ultrasonic testing, 1 day.*
19/1/55-12/2/55**LI**	*254,612 miles. Six modifications, four tests; boiler pressure reduced.*
27/4/56-16/6/56**GO**	*329,083 miles. Tender no.3347, 16/6/56. Rebuilt having run 329,083 miles, resited safety valves.*
11/5/57-24/5/57**LC**	*78,899 miles.*
5/12/57-11/1/58**LI**	*123,134 miles.*
17/2/58-22/2/58**NC-LC**	*124,184 miles.*
10/3/59-11/4/59**LI**	*210,233 miles.*
3/6/59-6/6/59**NC**	*213,047 miles. Five tests, 'T2296', bogie and coupled springs.*
5/10/59-10/10/59**NC**	*242,137 miles. BR type AWS fitted.*
22/9/60-15/10/60**LI-HI**	*294,501 miles, speedometer fitted.*
2/12/60-10/12/60**NC**	*314,000 miles.*
23/5/62-28/7/62**GO**	*397,016 miles.*
13/4/64-30/5/64**LI**	
30/12/65-11/1/66**NC**	
6/4/66-7/4/66**NC**	

Withdrawn May 1966 having run 903,542 miles. Stored at Weymouth shed 6-11/66 and then at Woodham Brothers, Barry 11/66-3/86. A number of years were spent in store on the Swanage Railway. It is now kept at Sellindge in Kent; the idea is to restore it to its original air smoothed casing condition.

Malachite green 35023 HOLLAND-AFRIKA LINE runs through Templecombe in early BR days. It did not lose its bonny SR livery until 1952, making it the last to run so. Photograph W. Hermiston, The Transport Treasury.

35023 HOLLAND-AFRIKA LINE

Entered traffic 6 November 1948 to order No.3393.
Named at Southampton Docks on 24/1/49 by Mr M.A. Pelt,
Managing Director of the Line.
For Tenders and Liveries - see separate Sections.

Boilers
1113
1092 10/54
1115 2/57
1102 11/62

Allocations
Exmouth Jct. 11/48
Bournemouth p/e 10/3/60
Weymouth p/e 17/10/66
Nine Elms p/e 17/4/67

Works: 1
22/2/50
20/9/50
18/2/52

Works: 2
(Mileages = since last General Overhaul)

11/4/53-2/5/53**LI**		
13/5/53-22/5/53**LC**	*Driving axle examined for flaws and replaced.*	
21/9/53-26/9/53**NC**		
10/5/54-29/5/54**NC**	*294,781 miles. Three modifications; boiler pressure reduced.*	
7/9/54-15/10/54**GO**	*306,964 miles. Fifteen modifications; resited safety valves.*	
28/11/55-31/12/55**LI**	*66,879 miles. Three modifications, 'T2274, 2282'.*	
19/11/56-1/12/56**LC**	*122,091 miles.*	
7/1/57-9/2/57**GO**	*126,952 miles. Seven modifications, five tests. Rebuilt having run 433,833 miles.*	
9/9/57-14/9/57**LC**	*177,700 miles. Three tests*	
22/4/58-10/5/58**LC**	*92,374 miles. Six tests.*	
3/2/59-28/2/59**LI**	*151,045 miles. 'T2283 and 2293'.*	
8/4/60-23/4/60**NC**	*220,361 miles.*	
4/7/60-7/7/60**NC**	*230,623 miles.*	
6/9/60-1/10/60**LI-HI**	*241,430 miles. AWS and speedometer fitted.*	
6/9/61-14/10/61**LC**	*295,908 miles. Spark arrester gear fitted.*	
5/12/61-16/12/61**NC**	*299,380 miles. 'T2341' new floorboards to diagram 52266.*	
20/9/62-17/11/62**GO**	*339,225 miles.*	
21/5/64-27/6/64**LI**	*'tests cancelled'.*	
30/3/66-12/5/66**HC**		

Withdrawn July 1967 having run 941,326 miles. Stored at Nine Elms shed 7/67-3/68 and scrapped at Buttigiegs, Newport in April, 1968.

Rebuilt 35023 HOLLAND-AFRIKA LINE (TIA box just visible on tender back) at Eastleigh 20 October 1957; it has picked up an earlier cast trailing truck at some point, in place of the fabricated one with which it would have started life. It is not always obvious but the two 'long' sand fillers in many – or maybe all – cases (such as this) are in fact a 'long' one for the rear wheel and a 'longer' one for the middle wheel. When made 'short' they were both 'short'. The joys of engine picking!
Photograph Les Elsey.

35023 at Exmouth Junction shed July 1957, headboard slightly awry. Photograph R.C. Riley

Exmouth Junction the following month;
HOLLAND-AFRIKA LINE this time
keeping company with ELDERS FYFFES.
Photograph W. Hermiston

35024 EAST ASIATIC COMPANY taking coal at Exmouth Junction, 21 May 1957. It got the coal-weighing tender nearly a year after this, and was rebuilt in April 1959. Photograph J. Robertson, The Transport Treasury.

35024 EAST ASIATIC COMPANY

Entered traffic 13 November 1948 to order No.3393.
Named at Waterloo station 5/5/49 by HRH Prince Axel of Denmark, Chairman of the Company.
For Tenders and Liveries - see separate Sections.

Boilers
1114
1097 5/54
1099 4/59

Allocations
Exmouth Jct 11/48
Bournemouth p/e 1/5/59
Nine Elms p/e 1/2/62
Weymouth p/e 14/9/64

Works: 1

17/1/49	*Ex-works 12/2/49*
21/2/49	*Done at Brighton (entered 2/3/49) where new BR blue was inspected by the Railway Executive.*
19/4/49	
22/6/50	
21/8/50	
23/4/51	

Works: 2
(Mileages = since last General Overhaul)

30/9/52-30/10/52	**I**	
12/5/53-22/5/53	**LC**	*Axle examined for flaws and replaced.*
5/4/54-15/5/54	**GO**	*289,428 miles. Sixteen modifications; boiler pressure reduced.*
4/7/55-30/7/55	**LC-HC**	*54,264 miles. Four tests.*
10/2/56-1/3/56	**LC**	*82,917 miles. One modification, four tests.*
6/9/56-29/9/56	**LI**	*118,639 miles. Seven modifications, five tests.*
19/11/57-14/12/57	**LI**	*195,951 miles. One modification, three tests.*
5/5/58-14/5/58	**LC**	*223,158 miles. Three tests.*
26/2/59-25/4/59	**GO**	*262,625 miles. Nine modifications, 'T2265'. Safety valves resited. Rebuilt having run 552,053 miles.*
13/10/59-20/10/59	**NC**	*35,594 miles. BR type AWS fitted.*
1/11/60-26/11/60	**LI**	*110,151 miles. Speedometer fitted.*
20/12/61-21/12/61	**LC**	*181,864 miles. Two tests*
7/6/63-27/7/63	**LI**	*249,685 miles. Spark arrester gear fitted, two tests.*

Withdrawn January 1965 having run 839,415 miles. Stored at Eastleigh shed 4/65 and scrapped at Woodfields, Town Dock, Newport, May, 1965.

Above. 35024 EAST ASIATIC COMPANY got the coal weighing tender when still in original condition and kept it when rebuilt – the engine's immaculate condition here at Eastleigh is because it has just emerged from works in the new guise. Photograph Les Elsey.

Below. 35025 BROCKLEBANK LINE, looking almost like a model, drifts down Honiton bank on 3 August 1955. It carries the new BR green and looks to be in beautiful condition. Though the new engines were by no means immune to slipping, the originals continued to demonstrate their extraordinary contradictions throughout the 1950s, to the wonder of observers. In the same year for instance, 1955, only a few days after this photograph and in wet conditions, 35022 slipped for *eleven miles* lurching between 26mph and 40mph; once it got a grip the engine suddenly tore away to nearly 90mph. The driver could not understand why anyone should be interested in such routine events and, genuinely puzzled, assured the *Railway Observer* correspondent that there was 'nothing wrong'. 'Curious engines!' wrote the correspondent... Photograph J. Robertson, The Transport Treasury.

35025 BROCKLEBANK LINE

Entered traffic 27 November 1948 to order No.3393.
Named at Waterloo station 20/9/49 by Colonel D.H. Bates, Chairman of the Company.
For Tenders and Liveries - see separate Sections.

Boilers
1115
1110 11/50
1104 12/56

Allocations
Bournemouth 11/48
Stewarts Lane p/e 25/3/50
Exmouth Jct. p/e 19/3/52
Nine Elms p/e 22/6/54
Bournemouth p/e 5/6/56
Exmouth Jct. p/e 10/3/60
Western Region stock 1/1/63

Works: 1
22/8/49
21/8/50
18/2/52

Works: 2
(Mileages = since last General Overhaul)

12/2/52-6/7/52**C**	
14/5/53-25/5/53**LC**	*Driving axle examined for flaws and replaced.*
21/9/53-17/10/53**HI**	*Boiler pressure reduced.*
3/5/54-8/5/54**LC**	*158,792 miles.*
4/1/55-5/2/55**LC-LI**	*183,159 miles. On 10 December, 1954 35025 had fractured the inside connecting rod, damaging the oil bath (as well as the track). The leaking oil set fire to the boiler lagging. Three modifications, 'T2242'; coupling rods, new pattern.*
6/4/55-22/4/55**NC-LC**	*193,780 miles. 'T2081, 2242'.*
30/12/55-21/1/56**LC**	*228,278 miles. 'T2081, 2242'.*
30/10/56-12/12/56**GO**	*258,749 miles. Rebuilt having run 419,374 miles; resited safety valves.*
9/7/57-13/7/57**NC**	*49,288 miles. Modifications to diagrams E30560 and E401; four tests. There followed a visit to Swindon Works Stationary Test Plant for investigatation into a 'knock' that had developed after running 35,000 miles.*
30/9/57-12/10/57**LC**	*59,235 miles. Steam chest pressure gauge pipe repositioned, cab handrails, left and right piston valve guide bushed; piston valve spindle at tail end; platform [the running board, that is] clearance for reversing screw grease nipple.*
12/11/57-23/11/57**LC-NC**	*63,155 miles. Five tests*
17/12/58-10/1/59**LI**	*127,340 miles. Two tests.*
22/10/59-31/10/59**NC**	*174,201 miles. BR type AWS fitted.*
30/5/60-25/5/60**LI**	*210,054 miles. ' T2305 driving coupling rod bushes, T2292 vacuum ejector cones, T2307 mechanical lubrication drive, T2282 boiler water gauge and drain cocks. Speedometer fitted.*
3/10/60-8/10/60**NC-LC**	*223,538 miles. Three tests.*
18/1/61-23/2/61**LC**	*(Exmouth Junction shed)*
15/11/61-16/11/61**LC-NC**	*298,057 miles. Three tests.*
17/1/62-10/3/62**GO**	*310,948 miles.*
26/7/63-14/9/63**LI**	*93,635 miles.*

Withdrawn in September 1964 after 884,081 miles. Stored at Exmouth Junction shed 2/65 and moved to Woodham Brothers, Barry in 3/65. Based on the GCR at Loughborough since February 1986 and undergoing long term restoration.

35025 BROCKLEBANK LINE transformed. Photograph The Transport Treasury.

BROCKLEBANK LINE, on the familiar Nine Elms 'Old Shed' roads, 8 July 1964. AWS fitted, but speedo definitely looks on its last legs. V.G. Gilchrist, in charge at Nine Elms at this time, wrote in March 1994 that the decision to rebuild the engines had been a mistake. He knew the engines before and after rebuilding; the originals in his care rarely lost time or failed and he never experienced a chain failure. He could detect no difference in coal consumption before or after rebuilding. This is horse's mouth stuff and cannot be ignored; the more one looks, the more it becomes clear that, as E.S. Youldon put it at the same time, 'the originals were nowhere near as bad as they were sometimes painted and the rebuilds not as wonderful...'
Photograph J.L. Stevenson, courtesy Hamish Stevenson.

35026 LAMPORT & HOLT LINE

Entered traffic 4 December 1948 to order No.3393.
Named jointly with 35028 at Southampton Docks 15/1/51 by Mr S.H. Mercer,
the London Manager of the Company.
For Tenders and Liveries - see separate Sections.

Boilers
1116
1103 1/57

Allocations
Bournemouth 12/48
Stewarts Lane p/e 25/3/50
Exmouth Jct. p/e 25/1/57
Bournemouth p/e 12/6/57
Exmouth Jct. p/e 1/5/59
Western Region stock 1/1/63
Nine Elms p/e 2/3/64
Weymouth p/e 14/9/64

Works: 1
20/6/49
18/12/50

Works: 2
(Mileages = since last General Overhaul)

13/5/52-14/6/52**I**		*Self cleaning smokebox fitted.*
9/1/53-31/1/53**C**		
8/6/53-13/6/53**LC**		*Driving axle replaced.*
21/9/53-16/10/53**LC**		
28/12/53-29/1/54**LI**		*207,669 miles. Modifications; 'T2133, casings at safety valve, T2195 self-cleaning smokebox gear, T2242 coupling rods MN class'.*
27/4/54-30/4/54**NC**		*219,303 miles. 'T 2133, 2194, 2242'.*
20/12/54-29/1/55**GO**		*245,662 miles. Seven modifications, two tests, modified balanced crank axle, boiler pressure reduced.*
11/5/56-2/6/56**LC**		*51,054 miles.*
13/12/56-26/1/57**GO**		*65,401 miles. Nine modifications, five tests, safety valves resited. Rebuilt having run 311,063 miles.*
9/8/57-24/8/57**LC**		*43,995 miles. Four tests.*
20/10/58-8/11/58**LI**		*128,908 miles.*
27/10/59-21/11/59**LI**		*205,051 miles. BR type AWS fitted.*
18/10/60-29/10/60**LC**		*274,182 miles. 'T2302'. Speedo fitted.*
14/3/61-15/4/61**LI-HI**		*299,853 miles.*
6/12/61-2/3/62**LC**		*(Exmouth Junction shed)*
29/8/62-20/10/62**GO**		*387,171 miles.*
13/3/64-17/4/64**NC**.		
28/9/65-5/11/65**LI**		
7/9/66-8/9/66**NC**		

Withdrawn in March 1967 having run 858,784 miles. Stored at Weymouth shed 4-8/67 and scrapped at J. Cashmore, Newport, September 1967.

35026 LAMPORT & HOLT LINE at Abbotscliff on 6 August 1956, during its spell on the Eastern Section 1950-1957. Photograph J. Robertson, The Transport Treasury.

35026 LAMPORT & HOLT LINE with the down Royal Wessex, south of Worting Junction, 3 August 1957. 35026 went to Exmouth Junction after its long spell on the Eastern Section in January 1957 until, with dieselisation in the west, it went to Nine Elms in the 1960s. In the meantime it had a couple of years at Bournemouth, from June 1957 to May 1959, and it was during this time that it worked the Royal Wessex, a Waterloo to Bournemouth and Weymouth (with M7s on to Swanage!) train, one of several special sets to mark the Festival of Britain of 1951. 35026 actually went to Bournemouth (along with 35021) for the accelerated two hour expresses of 1957. Photograph Les Elsey.

35027 PORT LINE at Nine Elms, attended by men above (trimming the coal) and below. This is 17 August 1956, with less than a year to go to rebuilding. Photograph J. Robertson, The Transport Treasury.

35027 PORT LINE

Entered traffic 11 December 1948 to order No.3393.
Named at Southampton Docks 24/4/50 by Mr W. Donald, Chairman of Port Line.
For Tenders and Liveries - see separate Sections.

Boiler
1117
1098 11/54
1101 5/57
1115 10/63

Allocations
Bournemouth 12/48
Stewarts Lane p/e 25/3/50
Bournemouth p/e 4/6/55

Works: 1
21/2/49
18/4/50
22/5/50

Works: 2
(Mileages = since last General Overhaul)

29/4/52-31/5/52**I**	
12/5/53-16/5/53**NC**	*Done at Ashford Works; driving axle examined for flaws.*
27/10/53-21/11/53**LI**	
6/5/54-8/5/54**LC**	*223,024 miles.*
15/10/54-26/11/54**GO**	*238,806 miles. Ten modifications and modified balanced crank axle. Boiler pressure reduced.*
26/8/55-3/9/55**LC**	*34,979 miles.*
3/4/56-28/4/56**LI**	*61,282 miles. Seven modifications, one test.*
28/3/57-10/5/57**GO**	*124,515 miles. Seven modifications, five tests. Rebuilt having run 363,351 miles, safety valves resited, new left-hand side cylinder.*
18/11/57-30/11/57**NC**	*52,446 miles. Six tests.*
7/1/59-24/1/59**LI**	*120,504 miles. 'T2282, 2292'.*
26/4/60-14/5/60**LI-HI**	*202,733 miles. AWS and speedometer fitted.*
6/10/61-4/11/61**LI**	*291,452 miles. 'T2305'.*
8/2/62-10/2/62**LC**	*298,480 miles. 'T2305'.*
24/8/62-19/10/62**LC**	*(Bricklayers Arms shed)*
9/8/63-5/10/63**GO**	*375,836 miles. Spark arrester fitted.*
3/9/65-15/10/65**LI**	

Withdrawn September 1966 having run 872,290 miles. Stored at Eastleigh shed 11/66-4/67 and at Woodham Brothers, Barry 5/67-12/82. When preserved went first to the Swindon & Cricklade Railway and was eventually restored at the old Swindon Railway Works. Currently based on the Swanage Railway.

Above. PORT LINE in straitened circumstances, leaving Southampton Central near the end of its working life, on 13 August 1966. Note the 5,100 gallon tender, No.3130 with the smaller vacuum tank cover, which it acquired instead of the large variety between July 1962 and August 1963. The tender survives today running with 34067 TANGMERE on the Mid-Hants Railway. Photograph J.L. Stevenson, courtesy Hamish Stevenson.

35028 CLAN LINE

Entered traffic 23 December 1948 to order No.3393.
Named at Southampton Docks 15/1/51 by Lord Rotherwick, Chairman of Clan Line.
For Tenders and Liveries - see separate Sections.

Allocations
Bournemouth 12/48
Dover p/e 29/10/49
Stewarts Lane p/e 25/3/50
Nine Elms p/e 14/6/59
Weymouth p/e 14/9/64
Nine Elms p/e 17/4/67

Boilers
1118
1120 12/54
1094 10/59
1121 2/64

Works: 1

1/1/51-13/1/51**NC**	*93,312 miles.*
30/1/51-28/2/51**LI**	*93,888 miles.*
24/9/51-20/10/51**HC**	*117,419 miles. New left-hand side cylinder.*
8/2/52-21/2/52**LC**	*128,856 miles.*

Works: 2
(Mileages = since last General Overhaul)

14/5/53-12/6/53**HI**	*167,052 miles.*
22/4/54-24/4/54**NC**	*199,651 miles. Trailing truck modified.*
25/10/54-3/12/54**GO**	*222,813 miles. 'T2132, boiler pressure reduced, resited safety valves.*
28/2/55-5/3/55**NC-LC**	*17,640 miles.*
19/9/55-24/9/55**LC**	*39,809 miles.*
5/6/56-7/7/56**LI-HI**	*65,605 miles. Six modifications.*
12/12/56-5/1/57**LC-HC**	*82,645 miles.*
6/8/58-6/9/58**LI**	*143,009 miles. Two modifications.*
21/8/59-24/10/59**GO**	*178,192 miles. Ten modifications, four tests,;BR type AWS fitted. Rebuilt having run 401,005 miles.*
2/6/61-28/7/61**LI**	*94,908 miles. Three tests, speedometer fitted.*
31/8/62-1/9/62**NC**	*152,100 miles. Three tests.*
13/3/63-7/5/63**LC**	*Done at Bricklayers Arms shop; 178,743 miles.*
4/12/63-1/2/64**LI-GO**	*210,376 miles. Spark arrester gear fitted, 'T2296, 2341'.*
20/9/65-21/10/65**LC**	*88,814 miles.*
12/7/66-21/7/66**LC**	*131,226 miles.*

Withdrawn July 1967 having run 794,391 miles. Purchased by Merchant Navy Locomotive Preservation Society straight out of service; since its first trip back on the main line in April 1974 has been one of the most consistent main line steam performers. Now fitted with air braking equipment and increased coal capacity. Has its own web site!

Mark Arscott writes: *'It was November 1965 that three enthusiasts first got together to plan the preservation of a Merchant Navy. The main requirement was £2,500, then a shortlist of engines that were in good order, both boiler and mechanical. 35022 was chosen and condemned almost immediately; second choice was 35028 laid up at the back of Nine Elms in February 1967 with a cracked Bissel truck. Fortunately Eastleigh decided to send a specialist welder to effect the repair, after which the loco returned to service. In the autumn of 1966 the artist David Shepherd was becoming interested in steam and preservation. Through his contacts with the Army and the Commanding Officer at Longmoor Camp, where the Army operated a large railway for training purposes, a berth was arranged for CLAN LINE and on 13 August 1967 she was duly towed to Liss for transfer to Longmoor. So began the engine's second life. It is interesting to note that the MNLPS have now owned 35028 for longer than BR ever did! Its exploits since have been well recorded. All contributions gratefully accepted.'*

Left. The last Merchant Navy to be rebuilt, 35028 CLAN LINE was ousted off the Eastern Section by the Kent Coast electrification. A few months before, on 13 June 1959, it was approaching Petts Wood with the down Golden Arrow, still with unmodified tender – the only one to get the later crest. Photograph Peter Groom.

CLAN LINE at Exmouth Junction on 17 August 1960. It was driven off, almost, into preservation with little thought that something like a third of the class would eventually rise from the dead (though some are far from fully 'alive' yet – give it time). Photograph W. Hermiston, The Transport Treasury.

That wonderful 'American' look of the Merchant Navys is demonstrated here, on the old Nine Elms roads on 12 May 1965. Tender is 5,100 gallons No.3129 which it had acquired in July 1952, its vacuum tank cover changing from the larger variety during 1959-61. Note the square cut-away faring to the front of the bunker roof, to aid coaling. 35029 ELLERMAN LINES, while truly covered in muck to a most undignified degree, still retains that look of limitless power, ready, it would seem, to spring away at an instant with that boiler of vast power. That wide firebox so responsible for the prodigious steam raising powers took/takes a ton of coal just to cover the grate in order to light up! Writes Mark Arscott, much involved early on in the preservation and running of CLAN LINE: *'This does not make them very popular on preserved lines – a truly caged lion!'* This was steam production on another level altogether really and, detail considerations aside, in the rebuilt Merchant Navys we might well have the apogee of Pacific power in this country. Tested in 1956, after one of the first rebuildings, the boffins could find hardly a trace of carbon monoxide in the smokebox of BIBBY LINE – indicating almost complete combustion. And yet, and yet. They were formidable things, certainly, but after conversion the odd point is that coal, in service, wasn't saved on a such a great scale as might have been expected. Even in ideal test conditions it was only around 10%. Photograph Alec Swain, The Transport Treasury.

35029 ELLERMAN LINES

Entered traffic 19 February 1949 to order No.3393.
Named at Southampton Docks 1/3/51 by Mr. A.F. Hull, Chairman of
Ellerman Lines.
For Tenders and Liveries - see separate Sections.

Boilers
1119
1122 12/54
1090 9/59
1103 11/63

Allocations
Bournemouth 2/49
Dover p/e 29/10/49
Nine Elms p/e 4/6/55
Weymouth p/e 14/9/64

Works: 1

22/2/50	*Repairs to tyres and wheel flanges damaged in derailment, London Bridge.*
18/12/50	*27/2/51 prepared at Eastleigh for naming ceremony at Southampton Docks.*
26/3/51	*Repainted to work train for Danish Royalty in May.*

Works: 2
(Mileages = since last General Overhaul)

11/6/52-11/7/52**I**	
3/7/53-10/7/53**HC**	
12/5/53-16/5/53**NC**	*Done at Ashford Works; driving axle examined for flaws.*
19/10/53-24/10/53**LC**	
28/10/54-4/12/54**GO**	*224,999 miles. Nineteen modifications, 'T2242, 2246'. Boiler pressure reduced and safety valves resited.*
25/4/56-26/5/56**LI**	*65,667 miles. Nine modifications.*
14/11/56-1/12/56**LC**	*93,453 miles. 'T2246'.*
30/7/57-24/8/57**LI**	*121,219 miles. Six modifications, 'T2207'.*
25/8/58-13/9/58**LC**	*181,115 miles.*
21/11/58-13/12/58**LC**	*190,401 miles. New right-hand side cylinder.*
27/2/59-28/3/59**LC**	*194,924 miles.*
30/6/59-19/9/59**GO**	*203,622 miles. Ten modifications, four tests; BR type AWS fitted. Rebuilt having run 428,621 miles.*
28/3/60-7/4/60**LC**	*38,091 miles. 'T2296, 2312, 2318'.*
8/5/61-3/6/61**LI**	*96,837 miles. Speedometer fitted, five tests.*
26/11/62-14/12/62**LC**	*177,167 miles. Three tests.*
10/9/63-9/11/63**LI-GO**	*208,458 miles. Spark arrester gear fitted.*
1/7/65-18/8/65**LC**	

**Withdrawn September 1966 having run 748,343 miles. Stored at
Weymouth shed 9/66-4/67 and at Woodham Brothers, Barry, 5/67-
1/74. Now a sectioned exhibit at the National Railway Museum York.**

**The last Merchant Navy emerged from Eastleigh in 1949. The next year 35030 ELDER DEMPSTER LINES, in sparkling
blue, was back at Eastleigh with nameplate covered up in readiness for the ceremony at Southampton Docks three days
later, on 5 June 1950. Photograph R.K. Blencowe Collection.**

35030 ELDER DEMPSTER LINES

Entered traffic 1 April 1949 to order No.3393.
Named at Southampton Docks 5/6/50 by Mr. G.H. Avezathe, a Director
of the Company.
For Tenders and Liveries - see separate Sections.

Boilers
1120
1113 10/54
1111 4/58
1122 5/62

Allocations
Bournemouth 4/49
Dover p/e 29/10/49
Nine Elms p/e 21/6/55
Weymouth p/e 14/9/64
Nine Elms p/e 17/4/67

Works: 1

18/4/50	*Repainted and cleaned for naming ceremony.*
18/6/51	*Ex-works w/e 30/6/51; fitted with indicator shelter.*
22/10/51	
22/2/53	

Works: 2
(Mileages = since last General Overhaul)

29/3/54-10/4/54**NC-LC**	*187,845 miles.*
20/9/54-22/10/54**GO**	*207,897 miles. Twelve modifications: boiler pressure reduced.*
1/12/55-14/12/55**LC**	*42,332 miles. 'T2204'.*
5/9/56-22/9/56**LI**	*79,586 miles. Seven modifications, 'T 2204'.*
12/3/58-23/4/58**GO**	*143,459 miles. Nine modifications, three tests, resited safety valves. Rebuilt having run 351,234 miles.*
12/5/59-23/5/59**LC**	*78,964 miles.*
12/5/60-28/5/60**LI**	*133,410 miles. AWS and speedometer fitted.*
11/1/61-28/1/61**LC**	*181,590 miles. 'T2285, Metcalf's steam heat couplings (new test)'.*
27/3/62-5/5/62**GO**	*230,583 miles.*
12/11/63-21/12/63**LI-HI**	*85,908 miles. Spark arrestor fitted, 'AWS gear made operative.'*

'To Eastleigh Works during period 7/2/66-5/3/66'.

Withdrawn July 1967 having run 850,876 miles. Stored at Nine Elms shed 7/67-4/68. Scrapped Buttigiegs, Newport, after storage there 5-12/68.

Power personified. The archetypal Merchant Navy view, at Waterloo, 23 June 1963. Photograph The Transport Treasury.